CW00547241

A Kitchen Equipped

Malcolm Harradine

ISBN 978-0-9569166-9-3. First published in November 2012 by Malcolm Harradine & Tabella Publishing LLP.

Layout and design by Tabella Publishing LLP. Printed in India by Imprint Digital Ltd.

For more information on this, or any of Malcolm's books, please visit his website:

www.melandmal.com

www.tabella.co.uk

A Kitchen Equipped

Malcolm Harradine

Contents

Foreword & about the author

FOREWORD

I consider myself very privileged to have been involved in the housewares industry for over 30 years, not only on the selling side but also in design and manufacturing. This has given me valuable insights into the thought processes and considerations that manufacturers go through when making a piece of cookware or kitchen equipment, as well as how it works and why an everyday cook in a domestic setting would want to buy it in the first place.

All too often I talk to consumers in stores who think they know what they want, but who are in great danger of spending a good deal of money on items that they don't really need. Cookware and kitchen equipment is a relative minefield, because there's so much on offer, so many variations of type, shape, and size.

I've been asked on hundreds of occasions why I don't write a book on the subject, so finally I thought, 'well ... why not?'

This book covers cookware, knives, and all manner of kitchen equipment, and will be equally useful to those starting out in a new home, as well as those who are replacing old for new many years on. You might sit and read the book cover to cover in one sitting (put the kettle on and make yourself comfortable!) but you can also dip into it to find specific information that is of interest to you. Either way, I hope you find it a worthwhile read. If it helps you to make a considered and well-informed decision, then I will have done my job.

ABOUT THE AUTHOR

Malcolm Harradine was 'knee height to a grasshopper' when he first discovered his love of cooking, with his Mum teaching him basic culinary skills on their farm in Hertfordshire. This love has never left him, and he is never happier than when he has a pan in his hand, concocting some new recipe or other.

In the early 1970s, after running the family catering business in Cornwall, Malcolm ventured into sales and marketing, which involved product development in both the catering and domestic kitchen sectors. Over the years he has seen a great many changes, both in technology and design, and today the kitchenware market is larger and more complex than ever.

In 2000, Malcolm began working as a professional in-store cooking demonstrator, and it was at that point, through talking to the general public, that it became apparent just how confusing the kitchenware market was. And so, this, his first book, *A Kitchen Equipped*, was conceived.

Nowadays, not only does he demonstrate kitchen equipment and offer his expertise in stores, Malcolm also appears at trade and consumer shows, carries out in-store training, provides training and sales videos, and also runs children's cookery classes, bringing the love of cooking to the youngsters of today.

In 1993, he first appeared on QVC TV Home Shopping Channel, and more recently moved to Ideal World Shopping TV, where he can be seen regularly introducing a wide range of the latest innovative kitchen products.

You can contact Malcolm through his website, www.melandmal.com, which also offers recipes, information and his own cookshop featuring his favourite, tried and tested, products.

Malcolm lives in Derbyshire with wife Melanie and their family, and, whenever time allows, enjoys a game of golf and disappearing into his workshop 'inventing recipes'!

ACKNOWLEDGEMENTS

My thanks go to my wife Melanie, for her unstinting support, and without whom this book would never have reached the printers. She is my rock.

To the many suppliers whom I have known for many years, for their generosity in allowing me to use their photographs to illustrate this, my first book: Chef Set Housewares, Easy Cook by Pendeford, George Wilkinson, Horwoods Housewares, JWP Ltd., Mastrad, Taylors Eye Witness, and last but not least, T&G Woodware.

And finally, a huge thank you to all the buyers, stores and staff & colleagues who have encouraged and supported me along the way.

Doing your homework

Many times, whilst I've been in-store doing a cooking demonstration, I've seen customers picking up one pan then another, and their facial expressions say it all – total confusion! It's hardly surprising, really, as there are so many brands, shapes, sizes, materials and weights.

There are many misconceptions as to what makes a good pan, and what you should look for when purchasing a new set of cookware, so it pays to do your homework before you spend your hard-earned cash! Ask yourself the following basic questions before you even set foot in the store:

• Which heat source do you cook on (hob): gas, electric, ceramic, induction, Aga or halogen?

• How many will you generally be cooking for, and do you entertain often?

• What is the budget for your new cookware?

• How much space do you have in your kitchen for storing cookware?

• Do you do any speciality cooking, such as Thai, Chinese, etc?

• Do you need your cookware to be dishwasher-safe?

There may also be other specific features that you need to consider, such as:

• Are you purchasing the cookware for somewhere other than the home: for a caravan or motorhome, for example, for use whilst camping, for a holiday home, or perhaps you're sending a child to university or college?

• Do you, or your partner (if he or she cooks) have any dexterity problems?

The answers to these questions will help you to focus on just what you need, not what you THINK you need – this will save you time and money in the long run, so it's certainly worth putting on your thinking cap!

HEAT SOURCES

Generally, most cookware will work perfectly well on gas or electric. The ones you have to watch out for are ceramic, Agas, and induction, as you will need specific cookware to get the best from them.

• Ceramic (glass top hobs with heat rings below the glass) need very flat-based cookware, so that the whole of the base touches the heat ring. Always look for cookware with smooth bottoms, as anything with a raised rough base will scratch the ceramic top. If the cookware has a smooth and flat base, it will be more effective for a ceramic hob.

Just one point with ceramic hobs – although cast iron (with a smooth base) is compatible, you do need to take care when placing the pan onto the glass top so as not to drop it and crack the glass (see my point regarding the weight of your cookware a little later).

• Agas need good thick bases. Manufacturers say a minimum of 3mm but I would recommend nothing less than 5mm, as the heat is so intense on an Aga, anything less will tend to warp in a short time. Therefore, go for heavy and good quality – and, as a lot of cooking is done within the Aga oven itself, you need cookware that will withstand high temperatures not only on the body of the pan and its lid, but also the knobs and handles.

• Induction was always a bit of a mystery in the early days of its development, and people tended to ignore how good it was. Furthermore, it was also hugely expensive to buy an induction hob, either a plug in or built-in version. However, due to its economic, energy-efficient, safety and easy-clean properties, this is rapidly becoming a firm favourite with consumers.

So, how does induction work?

The electro-magnetic coil beneath the toughened glass top of the hob produces a magnetic field, which 'attaches' itself to the compatible pan. This in turn is transferred to the pan, generating the heat.

Temperature control is instantaneous, you merely have to press the power button (+/-).

Electric	Radiant Ring	Ceramic / Halogen	Oven Safe Max 240°C	Gas	Induction	Diswasher Safe

Why induction?

In these energy-efficient times, induction is beyond doubt the most efficient way to cook. Heat is instant – as soon as you place your pan onto the hob, the magnetic current begins to work. You are losing (roughly) only 5% of the heat into the atmosphere, whereas, if you're using gas, you can say goodbye to 40%. Ceramic, as it works on heating the glass, loses even more. Induction is very reactive, changing from a fast boil to a gentle simmer at the touch of a button.

From a safety point of view, induction is fantastic, as the hob itself does not heat up directly – as I said before, it is the PAN and its contents that get hot, NOT the hob itself. So the moment you take the pan from the hob, the hob will switch off within a minute, with only residual heat from the pan itself remaining. So, if you have children or anyone elderly in the house and you're concerned about open flames, etc., induction is the safest form of heat source.

Furthermore, cleaning is an absolute doddle – just wipe over when you are finished.

What cookware do I need for an induction hob?

It's vital that you have induction-compatible cookware for it to work. Anything not magnetic (in the trade they call it a ferrous base) will not work

HOW MANY ARE YOU COOKING FOR?

If there are only one or two people in your household, then you are far better served buying smaller capacity pots and pans to avoid wasting valuable energy and money: larger pans are more expensive to purchase and heat up. However, if you have a large

on the induction hob, so the first thing you need is a fridge magnet. It sounds ridiculous but this is the easiest way you can test which pans are compatible – although cookware manufacturers usually state clearly on the packaging that their cookware is for use on an induction hob.

Simply hold the magnet to the base of the pan (not the side or top) and, if it sticks, it will work. It always makes me laugh when I see couples in kitchen departments secretly holding a fridge magnet in their palms and trying to stick it to the bottoms of pans! Remember to remove the magnet before placing the pan on the hob top – I once had a customer come back complaining that the pan I'd sold him didn't lay flat on the hob top and it wouldn't work as a result. I wonder why!

If you want to see a video of how an induction hob works, log on to my website www.melandmal.com and visit 'Videos'.

family to cater for, or do a lot of entertaining, then obviously go for the larger capacity.

WHAT DO I NEED?

The most popular sizes of saucepans are 14cm (often called a milk pan), 16cm, 18cm and 20cm. Add a frying pan (with or without lid) and you have the basic requirements to cook a substantial meal for you and your family.

I would highly recommend a graduated multisteamer unit, with staged sides so that it will fit onto either a 16, 18 or 20cm pan. You then use the lid from the 20cm pan on the steamer part itself. This means that you are only using one ring on your hob to cook two things, for example, potatoes in the bottom and vegetables in the steamer compartment, so it's more energy efficient.

YOUR BUDGET

Everyone has a budget, of course, and if yours is restricted, rather than purchasing five low budget pans, go for three better quality pans for the same price. These will give you better long-term service and superior cooking results. However, there are exceptions to this rule! One is with regard to buying cookware for the offspring for university life; when it's needed for only three to five years, longevity isn't really an issue. Plus, let's face it, the students' kitchen is usually a war zone! I clearly remember giving my daughter some very good quality pans when she entered university, but after one term they were totally unrecognisable, and fit only for the dustbin after her three-year degree course! Naturally, she blamed the other students for the demise of her cookware!

Another exception is when buying for a second home, maybe a holiday home, caravan or motorhome, or for camping. Weight may be more important in these situations, and less expensive may be fine as it's not being used on a daily basis. A couple of decent-sized saucepans and the obligatory frying pan will do the trick; non-stick being a good idea if no dishwasher is available.

HOW MUCH SPACE DO YOU HAVE FOR STORAGE? Think about where you're going to store your cookware when it's not in use – there's no point buying things that simply won't fit into your cupboards. Some manufacturers have addressed this problem, and have introduced nesting pans where three sizes of pans with their lids on nest inside one another. This is a really clever idea, and perfect if you have very limited space or have a motorhome or caravan where space really is of a premium. Usually, pans will sit inside each other, but with the lids removed and stacked, and this tends to suffice if you only have one cupboard or shelf to store them in. Alternatively, you could buy a rack to house your pans, either the type that stands on your worktop or on the floor, or hangs from the ceiling. This will free up cupboard space for other things.

DO YOU DO ANY SPECIALITY COOKING? If you enjoy cooking Chinese, Indian, Thai or Mediterranean food on a regular basis, then you may find that you need specific cookware to the job properly.

• Chinese, Indian and stir-fry cooking needs the traditional wok. The best in my opinion are made from good quality carbon steel, and are relatively inexpensive and conduct heat very quickly. You'll see stainless steel and non-stick woks in the stores, but I far prefer carbon steel. It isn't as pretty, but boy, does it do a good job! Wherever possible, try to buy a flat-bottomed wok as this will be suitable for most hob types.

• Size-wise, it depends how many you're cooking

for, but in general, a medium-sized wok – about 32-36cm in diameter – will probably be large enough to feed four to six people, and will be easy enough to store in your cupboard.

• Spanish paella pans are readily available in a variety of sizes (my suggestion would be a 38cm diameter) but the main feature is that they are quite shallow and have sloping sides which helps the rice to cook evenly. They tend not to come with lids as the Spanish way is to cook in an open pan.

- My favourite, and very well used 38cm paella pan, is made from carbon steel, but you can buy them in stainless steel or enamelled versions.

DISHWASHER VERSUS HAND WASHING
Later, I'll go into much more detail regarding the care and use of your cookware, but first of all, the question I always get asked: will this cookware go in a dishwasher?

Personally, I would rather wash my pans by hand – it's quicker and doesn't take up all the space in the dishwasher. Many manufacturers now promote the fact that you can put their cookwares into a dishwasher, but if you're adamant that you do NOT want to wash your cookware by hand, then you need to be aware of certain types of metal that must be avoided: anodized and aluminium. These two types are definite dishwasher no-nos, as the salts in the washer are attracted to the surface of these metals and distort the appearance, practically 'eating' into the pan and pitting the surface. More about this (and aluminium and anodized cookware) later.

DEXTERITY AND WEIGHT
It goes without saying that if whoever's using the cookware has dexterity problems, perhaps through arthritis, or is unable to lift any great weight, then the lighter the cookware the better. This doesn't mean that it has to be cheap; it just means that the cookware needs to be made from a lighter metal, such as aluminium. In all metal cookware, it tends to be the bases that carry the weight, with the exception of cast iron cookware which looks beautiful but is so heavy even before it has anything put in it. Always consider the weight of the pan being filled with potatoes before you buy it!

So, now you've asked yourself these questions, and answered them honestly, let's move on to the next stage … purchasing cookware for your kitchen …

Cookware – pots & pans

Hopefully, having done your homework in Chapter 1, you'll have a better idea of what cookware you need, so now let's go through the general types of cookware that you will see in your local stores, and talk about the main features and benefits of each.

STAINLESS STEEL

Stainless steel is an extremely robust material, and it's easy to think that ALL stainless steel pans are so. However, it's all down to the thickness of the metal. Here are a few tips:

• When comparing the relative thicknesses of pan bodies, tap them with the edge of a coin (gently, so as not to damage them!). The higher the pitch, the thinner the metal – you're looking for a baritone clunk! For quality and strength, the pan body should not be less than 0.8mm thick.

• Look for pan bodies with rolled edges at the top, as this form of manufacturing also increases the strength of the pan and denotes a better quality.

• Stainless steel is a very poor conductor of heat. If a pan was constructed solely from pure stainless steel, cooking would be erratic due to temperature differences across the base of the pan (hot spots), causing burning. To prevent this, manufacturers incorporate alternative (better heat-conducting) metals, such as copper or aluminium, into the base of their pans. This is known as an encapsulated base in the trade – but put simply, a slab of aluminium (or copper) is sandwiched between the base of the pan and a stainless steel plate. Now, when the pan is placed onto the hob, the heat is conducted straight to the aluminium part of the base. The encapsulated base will ensure that the pan heats very quickly, and also gives superb heat distribution across the whole of the base. This, in turn, will greatly reduce the possibility of food sticking or burning to the inside of the pan.

Tri-ply

Tri-ply cookware is a three layer constructed cookware, comprising an outer layer of stainless steel, a middle layer of aluminium, followed by another layer of stainless steel – in effect, an aluminium sandwich! This makes for extremely efficient performance as well as excellent heat distribution and retention throughout the whole pan.

ALUMINIUM

There are three types of aluminium cookware on the market, basic aluminium being the first, so let's start with that ...

Basic aluminium

This metal has served the cookware industry well for many years, is greatly loved, and is still used by caterers as it's inexpensive, light, durable, and gives an even heat distribution, second only to copper. In the High Street, you'll generally find aluminium cookware not in its basic catering form, i.e. the uncoated version, but usually with a coloured enamel exterior and a non-stick interior. As a rule of thumb, the body of the pan should not be less than 2mm thick – the packaging will tell you this.

The enamel outer protects the soft aluminium from everyday knocks, and doesn't stop the excellent heat distribution, so you get both strength and performance in one.

Aluminium in its basic form is very prone to sticking if you don't season it beforehand. If you have a basic catering pan, you have to oil and salt it each time you use it, which is a bit of a bind in a domestic situation usually, so always look for non-stick coating inside the pans.

Handles and knobs are usually made from phenolic resin, which is heat-resistant high density plastic – but more about this later.

Cast aluminium

Casting is when the aluminium has been heated to form a molten liquid and is then poured into moulds. The advantage of this method is that the thickness of the metal is consistent throughout the vessel, giving exceptional heat distribution and no hot spots. The downside is that it is a very expensive form of manufacturing, and this is reflected in the price, but if you're looking for quality, performance and durability, you can't go far wrong with cast aluminium.

Hard anodized aluminium

Aluminium is a softer metal than stainless steel, but with modern technology, manufacturers have made it almost twice as robust as stainless steel, having cleverly changed the molecular structure to harden the surface of the aluminium (whilst retaining the superb heat distribution, so the best of both worlds).

Without getting too scientific, this is aluminium cookware which, during manufacture, undergoes a process which makes the surface of the aluminium very hard. The surface is then given a high quality non-stick coating which attaches itself to the anodized aluminium surface to give excellent durability and performance.

My wife always says it seems a very masculine sort of cookware range, being grey or black in colour with an almost semi matt finish to it. This is her personal opinion, of course, and she is more interested in how it looks rather than what it does, but I can tell you that our hard anodized frying pan of many years is still used almost on a daily basis, and is still as good as new. The only disadvantage, for some, is that it cannot go in a dishwasher as the salts erode the surface, so it's into the sink with anodized I'm afraid!

CAST IRON

Cast iron is suitable for all heat sources, including induction, but it's particularly good for Aga cooking as it will withstand very high temperatures. Because it retains the heat so well, you need only cook on a low to medium heat to maintain an even cooking temperature, so it's extremely energy efficient.

It's important that you check that the base of the cookware is absolutely flat when using on induction and/or ceramic hobs, as the whole of the base needs to be in contact with the heat to ensure maximum heat distribution and avoid hot spots.

In its basic form, cast iron does not have any non-stick lining so will need seasoning on a regular basis – this means that you need to oil the pan every time you use it, and only wipe it clean after use, rather than washing it up. Seasoning it will build up a non-stick coating.

If this is not an option for you, you can buy cast iron cookware which has a vitreous enamel coating inside, giving a smooth, glass-like finish. This makes the pan non-stick and, therefore, easy clean. The outside of the pan is coated with a coloured enamel which protects the pan from rusting and scratching glass hob tops, but you'll pay a premium for this as the manufacturing process is quite lengthy and expensive.

Good quality cast iron fry and griddle pans usually have a black enamel coating, which simply means that you don't have to oil before use.

The only downside with cast iron cookware is the weight. So, when you're picking up the pans in store, make sure you take into consideration how heavy the item will be when full of food!

Induction-friendly cookware

In the past, any mild steel, enamel and cast iron worked on an induction hob as these materials have a natural 'magnetic base'. However, due to the dramatic rise in the sales of induction hobs, manufacturers of stainless steel and aluminium pans now add in a ferrous base during the manufacturing process, which makes these two popular metals compatible with induction cooking. Check the packaging on the pan, though – if it's induction-friendly, it will state this quite clearly; and, of course, get out your magnet!

Pure cast iron cookware is perfect for induction, with the only disadvantage that it does have a rough base so it would be better to lift the pan from the glass hob top rather than dragging it, in case it scratches the surface. Cast iron is great to cook with as it conducts the heat so quickly, but it's also very heavy, so avoid it if you have limited hand strength.

NON-STICK INTERIORS

Teflon and DuPont are the names that most of us associate with good quality non-stick.

The quality of non-stick is gauged by how many layers are coated onto the pan, from one to three coats. The more coats it has, the thicker the non-stick, and the longer it will last. However, the actual durability of the non-stick is governed by the thickness of the pan itself. If the pan is of an inferior quality, and very thin, it will be prone to 'hot spots', and it is these that weaken the non-stick coating, no matter how good the non-stick is. So,

you need thickness of the pan AND non-stick, so check out the gauge of metal used in the pan – good manufacturers give you this information on the packaging.

To maintain the non-stick for many years, the rule is to always cook on a lower heat – if you want to sear a piece of steak, then do so very quickly on a high heat, then turn it down. Non-stick does NOT like overheating for long periods of time, as it causes the surface to lift and peel off, even on the best non-stick linings.

When I was a Sales Director for a cookware company back in the 1990s, I was called to the Quality Control Department to give my opinion on a return from a customer. I don't know what I was expecting to see, but a frying pan with a burnt on, almost blackened egg stuck to the centre of it was not it! When we had all stopped laughing about the fact that someone would send a pan back with the egg still attached, it became very clear that the customer had turned the heat up so high, the egg and, most importantly, the non-stick surface, hadn't stood a chance, and this was clear on the base and sides of the pan which had turned a yellow hue – always a sign of heat abuse. We sent the customer another pan anyway as a gesture of goodwill, but I have to say that I have never had a return like that since!

Do not use metal utensils on a non-stick surface, as these will inevitably scratch the surface and render your non-stick 'not so non-stick' very quickly. Use plastic, silicone or wooden cooking utensils, and the quick release surface will last much longer. Remember, though, that non-stick does not last forever, but with good practice, it will certainly give several years of service.

HOB TO OVEN – DUAL USE

Dual use items mean you can cook on the hob first, and then place them into the oven – to brown the top or finish the cooking, for example. There's no need to transfer the food to another pot, thus saving on washing up! For example, you might be making a casserole, searing meat and onions then adding other ingredients on the hob top, then want to finish it off or cook it slowly in the oven – no problem. Just pop on the lid and put the whole lot in. This alleviates the need to buy separate casserole pots and dishes – a good-sized saucepan will do the trick, and, as an added bonus, having the handle on the pan makes it easier to remove it from the oven.

However, you may prefer to have an actual casserole pan, of the same construction as a saucepan, that you can use on the hob top itself, but with handles at each side rather than just a long pan handle. More about this option a little later on.

Just to be on the safe side, it's worth checking the maximum temperatures the cookware can handle, usually around 220°C, but some can withstand temperatures to 240°C.

LIDS

Most standard saucepans come with a lid, generally in the same metal as the pan, or made from clear, toughened glass.

Stainless steel or aluminium lids are preferred by chefs, as they are very robust and can endure the same maximum temperature in the oven as the pan.

Toughened glass lids are generally made with a stainless steel rim to give more strength. The advantage with this type of lid is that you can see what is happening in the cooking process without having to take off the lid. They are designed to

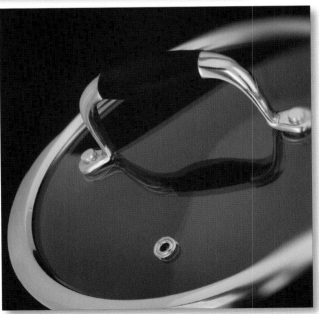

handle oven temperatures of up to 180°C, but the downside is that they can shatter if dropped, and are generally much heavier that stainless steel lids.

You can also buy cookware with self draining lids. These incorporate small side holes on one side for draining pasta or rice, and larger holes on the opposite side for draining vegetables. Simply hold the lid in place and pour off the liquid. This obviates the need for a colander.

HANDLES AND KNOBS

It's all very well talking about the type of material the cookware is made from, but you mustn't forget about handles and knobs, as these are also very important. As you peruse the huge choice of cookware, you'll find some with black knobs and handles, and some with stainless steel. So, which ones are best?

Basically, there are three types of handles that are fixed to the pan body: phenolic, stainless steel, and cast stainless steel, and these are fixed with screws, riveted, or are spot welded into position.

Phenolic is a solid resin material, known as Bakelite in the good old days, very lightweight and very durable. The handles are attached to the pan body using a bracket, which is first spot welded to the pan body. A metal ferrule or cover is added which conceals the bracket and reduces heat transfer to the handle. Finally, the handle itself is screwed through the ferrule into the bracket. This method gives extra strength to the handle and makes it secure.

The knob is also usually attached to the lid using a screw, so you may find that over time the inner screw in both the handle and knob may work a little loose and will need to be retightened using a screwdriver. I can remember my Dad doing this in days gone by!

Phenolic is a poor conductor of heat, so will stay much cooler when in use on the hob, although you must take care not to have the heat too high as the handles do hold residual heat if the flame laps up around them. If you put the lid on the pan, the knob will get warm, but usually only mildly (just warm to the touch). If in doubt, and until you get used to your new cookware, wear an oven mitt!

Phenolic is ovenproof up to 180°C, so you can start the cooking on the hob top but finish off the dish in the oven. However, if you do put the cookware in the oven, you will need oven gloves to remove both the pan itself and the lid, as the surrounding heat from the oven is so much more intense than on a hob top.

Stainless steel handles are light, and are attached to the pan either with small stainless steel rivets or by spot welding directly onto the pan itself. You can tell if a handle or knob has been spot welded as you will see four small marks on the inside of the pan or lid due to the heat from the welding. Riveting is self explanatory, in that the handles and knobs are held onto the pan via stainless steel rivets, and again, you will see these on the inside of the pan or lid.

Stainless steel handles and knobs can get quite warm in use, as they're made from a thinner metal and the heat tends to travel through them, so oven mitts are a must when removing the pan from the heat.

Stainless steel handles and knobs are ovenproof up to 240°C.

Cast stainless steel has become the preferred type of material for handles and knobs, as it does not get hot. The handles are generally attached to the pan by spot welding or rivets, and incorporate a 'V' shape between the handle and the pan body

to allow heat to disperse rather than travelling into the handle itself. The downside is that the handles are much heavier, so you may want to take this into consideration if you have difficulty lifting.

Without doubt, handles and knobs which are riveted into place using stainless steel are by far the most resilient, as riveting gives the pan strength and durability; the rivets become part of the pan body itself. It's highly unlikely that the handle will come away from the pan body, even if exposed to the highest heat and maximum use. No wobbly bits here!

Finally, with technology always moving forward, and the popularity of everything silicone, you may often now find this material inlaid into handles and

knobs. This keeps the heat down, protects the hands, and makes the handle non-slip, important if you have dexterity problems.

SHOULD I BUY A SET OR GO FOR LOOSE PIECES?
It goes without saying that sets always offer better value, compared to the cost of buying all the pieces separately. However, do not fall into the trap of buying a set if there is any doubt that you would not use ALL the pieces. Years ago a relative of mine purchased a set of cookware at what seemed to be a very good price, but it was only when she came to use them that she realized she was never going to use that egg poacher, and would have been better served by a frying pan instead. She then had to spend more money buying the item that she really needed in the first place.

So what do I really need?
It's the question I am constantly asked and I always say the same thing – go for the basics to get you started:

- One of each of the standard sizes of saucepans – 16, 18, 20cm.

- A good non-stick frying pan.

- A large sauté pan with lid.

- A multi steamer.

Three basic pans – 16, 18 and 20cm saucepans with lids – are great for everything, from warming your baked beans to cooking a large pan of potatoes for the family. Just as a note, if you struggle with lifting heavy weights, for example a pan full of potatoes, then it might be worth buying the largest pan with a helper handle, an extra lifting handle on the opposite side to the long handle, to help even out the weight. You can use both hands, then, when removing the pan from the heat.

A frying pan, preferably non-stick, around 28-30cm; perfect when cooking your Sunday morning fry up, and for everyday use.

A large sauté pan with lid, around 28-30cm –

invaluable when you need a little more depth to the pan, for example when you're making a Bolognese or curry (and if you buy the same size as the frying pan, you can use the one lid on both pieces).

A non-stick omelette pan is a must: around 20cm – great for cooking a decent-sized omelette, or when you're cooking smaller quantities of food, such as fried eggs and bacon.

A graduated multi-steamer with the base staged to fit all of your saucepans. Just pop it on top of any one of your saucepans, use the lid on top of the steamer section, and hey presto! This means you can cook two things on only one ring – space saving and energy efficient.

Of course, you can always add more to your collection as time goes on, but this is a good start, and you'll cover the basics with these six items. More about stage two and beyond later!

My recommendation would always be to visit a good kitchenware department or cookshop and actually pick up the pans, feel the weight, and check out the handles and knobs, etc., for yourself. By all means shop around for the best offers, it would be foolish not to as it's a very competitive market, but go armed with the facts and in the knowledge that, when you do part with your hard-earned cash, it will buy you a set of cookware that you really, really want.

If you avoid a cheap economy set, they should last a good many years. I'll be touching on the subject of how to treat your pans properly later on in this section, but for now the adage "… you get what you pay for" is true. Buy the best pans that you can afford – or buy one good quality pan to begin with, and add another to your collection when you can afford it.

However, saying that, there are a couple of exceptions to the rule! Although I have dedicated

a whole chapter (Chapter 10) to adding to your collection, there are two extra pieces of cookware that may be useful additions, and worth mentioning here. If you make stews, soups, or larger quantities of food in one go and need something fit for that purpose, then a casserole pan and/or a large stock pot would be worth thinking about.

CASSEROLES

There is a huge array of ceramic dishes available, in all shapes and sizes – the sort of thing you can put in the oven and then take straight to the table. However, in most cases you'll have to use a pan to start the cooking process; for example, searing the

meat, frying off onions, etc., before transferring into the cooking pot itself. This is because these ceramic dishes don't have bases suitable for use on direct heat (they will crack, and all your lovingly prepared food will end up all over your hob top – very messy!).

I've already mentioned using a normal saucepan with a long side handle to do all the pre-oven cooking stuff, adding the other ingredients, and then transferring it to the oven to finish it off, but you may prefer to have a casserole pan instead; these are neater, and have rounded handles (stainless steel or phenolic) on both sides.

These casseroles are constructed with a thick base (like that of a saucepan) so you can use them on the hob top, and they'll withstand the high temperatures in the oven (always check the maximum temperature the particular casserole pan can go up to). The difference is in the handles, and the fact that they may fit more easily into your oven. Furthermore, if you're likely to be cooking in large quantities, which means the vessel will be heavier, then it's easier and safer to move from hob-to-oven with two handles, as the weight is distributed evenly.

Most cookware manufacturers incorporate a range of casseroles into their ranges, from as small as 16cm in diameter to around 26cm. In my opinion, there's little point buying a small casserole, as a saucepan would do the same job and would fit into your oven with ease. Spend money on this small size item and you're merely doubling-up on what you already have in your cupboards. However, if you're cooking in larger quantities, then it's worth considering the sizes beyond the diameter of your basic saucepans.

When choosing a casserole, bear in mind the size of your oven. Don't do, as my wife did once, when preparing food for a large gathering. She rummaged through my samples looking for the biggest pot she could find, did all the necessaries on top of the hob, and then tried to get it into the oven, only to find it was too wide and too tall! Then, she had to find a casserole that would not only hold the quantity but also fit the oven! Size is also a major consideration if you only have a small oven or use a combination oven/microwave.

You should also consider the weight of the casserole pan once filled, especially if you usually prepare larger amounts of food. You may find that you can't lift it off the hob top in the first place!

I'd recommend that you go for one no larger than 24cm, around four litres in capacity, as this size will fit in most ovens, and you'll be able to move it from hob-to-oven without too much trouble.

Casserole pans are not just for making stews or for hob-to-oven use: they are multi-use, which is what makes them worth considering. In our kitchen we use them to cook pasta and rice, potatoes and larger vegetables, such as cabbage, which, uncooked, take up a lot of space and need to be cooked in larger volumes of water, or when a 'normal' sized saucepan is just not large enough.

Basically, if you take my advice and initially buy the three sizes of saucepans referred to earlier, by adding a 24cm casserole pan, either at the same time or later on, you will have enhanced your collection, not cluttered it up!

STOCK POTS

There may be occasions when you need a deeper or taller piece of cookware. This is particularly relevant if you need to use a good amount of liquid in the cooking. For example, if you regularly make stocks

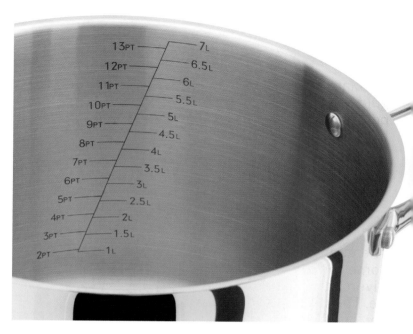

using a chicken carcass or fish pieces, or if you want to boil the salt out of a large piece of gammon, or want to slow cook a complete joint of meat on the hob top.

Like the casserole, a stock pot is made exactly as a saucepan, with an encapsulated base, and generally comes with two rounded side handles for easy lifting. Department stores and cookshops will offer stock pots from 22cm to 26cm in diameter, and, in the catering industry, they're available right up to 36cm! For a domestic kitchen, my advice would be to opt for one around 24cm in diameter (approximately 5-6 litres). Any bigger and you would need the muscles of Atlas to lift it off the hob!

In a domestic kitchen, stock pots are generally used on the hob top only, as they're too tall for the oven (but then stocks and soups don't need to see the inside of the oven anyway).

We have a stock pot at home that we use regularly to make soups throughout the year, but our favourite use for it is on Bonfire Night when my wife always makes a mega chilli for the ever-growing number of friends and family who turn up for our regular 5th of November event. She just cooks it all in the stock pot from scratch, then my job is to move it outside onto the barbeque to keep it warm (not that it lasts long enough to go cold in the first place!).

Another use for a stock pot is for wine making. A friend borrowed ours when he first began making wine, and ended up buying his own as it did the job perfectly. Jam makers, though, should consider investing in a maslin pan, which will also suffice for wine making (see Chapter 10 for more about maslin pans).

Many manufacturers have added a measuring guide to the inside of their casseroles and stock pots, so you can fill the pan with the liquid required, before adding the ingredients (no need for a measuring jug).

These two items are certainly worth considering, but only if you're going to use them more than once a year.

MANUFACTURERS' GUARANTEES

The guarantees that good manufacturers offer, some for ten years, some for a lifetime, are not given lightly, and are regulated by the powers that be. The well-known cookware companies spend serious amounts of cash testing, testing, testing their cookware in extreme scenarios so that they're confident that their cookware will last the course. I remember visiting a well-known cookware factory in Portugal, and being amazed at how rigorously random samples from each batch were put through their paces – there were machines to scratch the surfaces, burn the bases, and stress the handles – and nothing left the factory until it was 100%.

This reinforced my confidence that if the guarantee states 'lifetime' on the box, with careful use it means just that. Equally, if it says 'five-year guarantee' on the box, then don't expect it to last forever.

CARING FOR YOUR COOKWARE

Buying a new set of cookware is like getting a new car ... you look after it religiously for the first few

months then the novelty wears off, and before you know it there are rust spots and scratches, and it really isn't looking too good anymore.

I know it's a pain, and you will grimace at me when I impart this bit of news, but ... if you look after your cookware, it will look after you.

Contrary to popular belief, stainless steel IS easy to clean! Some stainless steel pans have a non-stick interior, but consider that the best chefs in the world use plain stainless steel pans and never have anything sticking to their bases! It's all about treating the cookware with respect – keeping the heat low to medium will prevent food burning on the base or sides. I always say, "Let the pan do the cooking, not the flame."

To clean stainless steel cookware, simply use warm soapy water and a mild scourer, rinse and wipe with a dry cloth.

If you do use too high a heat (and let's be honest,

we all do it) and it leaves a black mark, just bring some water and a splash of lemon juice or vinegar to the boil, turn down the heat and let it simmer for 10 minutes. This will release the mark, and you can then just wash the pan as normal.

Looked after in this way your cookware will remain looking good for years to come. If you want to go one step further, particularly if you leave your cookware out on show, there are plenty of stainless steel cleaners on the market.

Cleaning anything with a non-stick interior is a doddle – just wash in warm soapy water with a dish cloth – scourers should be avoided and are unnecessary anyway, because, if the non-stick is a good one, nothing will adhere to it.

To dishwash or not to dishwash – that is the question

Dishwashers are wonderful things – having had one in our kitchen for many years makes me wonder how we ever managed without one! However, I still like to wash my cookware by hand, much to the chagrin of my wife who tuts every time I pile up the pans on the counter top and run a sink full of soapy water!

Now, don't get me wrong – you CAN put certain types of cookware into your dishwasher, as long as the manufacturer says so, but the high temperatures, cleaning abrasive and salts used in a dishwasher will eventually take their toll on your beautiful set of cookware. Call me old fashioned, but I cannot see the point in filling it up with large pieces of cookware: plates, china, crockery, glasses – yes; pans, steamers, frying pans – no. It's far easier to wash them by hand, and, in my opinion, better for the cookware too.

It's a bone of contention in our house, which I guess will always be the case – 'er indoors on one side of the fence, me on the other (or on it probably!).

So ... that covers all the basics, and you'll now be able to make an informed decision when you step into that High Street store or investigate on t'internet.

Simply, be clear in your mind what you would like and why, and how much your budget will stretch to. Don't be tempted to veer off your chosen path or be swayed by fancy packaging or a very persuasive sales advisor!

If you have any specific questions, you are more than welcome to visit me on my website: www. melandmal.com.

Knives & accessories

There is no doubt that every kitchen needs a selection of good knives, and the type and quality of the knives you buy will be one of the most important decisions you'll make when equipping your kitchen.

When you think about it, we use knives for just about everything during food preparation, from peeling carrots to filleting fish, chopping herbs and slicing Sunday roast. We would be pretty much lost without them!

Having used knives professionally for many years, and even being entrusted to present them on live television on various shopping channels (I think they thought there was less chance of me cutting off my finger with a live audience watching!), I know exactly which knife will be best for a given job. However, if you don't have much experience with knives, knowing which to use can be very confusing. There are so many to choose from, so many variations in shape and size, and such a range of prices. This section will help de-mystify knives, and allow you to go out there and choose your knives confidently.

These days you can buy gadgets to chop apples, eggs and bananas, and to slice cabbage, carrots and potatoes, but the simple facts are that these gadgets won't get used very often, and washing them is time consuming. They'll end up taking up valuable space in your kitchen cupboards, and never see the light of day again! A knife will do the job just as well, if not better, so why waste your money? It's far more sensible to invest in a few good knives.

I was once asked what three things I would take to a desert island. "Easy," I said confidently, "I would take my chef's knife, my halogen oven, and, of course, my wife," thinking that would earn me some Brownie points when she heard it. Instead, I got it in the neck from the interviewer (a woman) for putting my wife as third choice! The moral of the story, choose your knives carefully, but be careful about where you put your wife in the pecking order!

Anyway, back to the subject in hand ...

Knives aren't recent inventions – it's almost three million since Mr. Stone Age used a piece of flint lashed to a stick to cut up his meat! Thankfully, we have moved on a bit since then. The first metal to be used was copper, followed by bronze, which is an alloy of tin and copper. Then along came iron, which had both strength and weight, and then iron was mixed with carbon to create steel. However, steel, of course, is prone to corrosion and rusting, but when chromium was added to the steel that solved those problems, and gave us the stainless steel we know today.

To fully appreciate the differences you will find in prices in the High Street, and, therefore, an

indication of the quality, you need to understand how knives are manufactured. I don't want to get bogged down in the science involved, but, basically, there are two types of knife: forged and stamped.

Forged knives go through many processes, some done by humans rather than machines, hence their more expensive price label. They are made from a single piece of steel where the blade and the tang (the bit that is attached to the handle) are in one piece. All forged knives have a bolster, a bulge that you will see between the handle and the blade. This is not added separately but is formed by placing the knife into intense heat, then pushing both ends of the knife toward each other, causing this bulge to appear. To develop the strength of the knife and, in

particular, the blade, the knife is heated and rapidly cooled many times then hammered to remove any imperfections or distortions, before grinding. The blade is ground and polished before the handle is fitted, and finally the knife is sharpened to a fine finish.

Going through this rigorous process ensures that forged knives are very high quality, very strong, need less sharpening, and will last a lifetime if treated with care. They really are the crème de la crème of knives, but you'll need to dig deep into your wallet if you want a set!

Machine stamped knives are processed in a much less costly way, so there are many more on offer in the High Street, and, more importantly, at prices that will perhaps better suit your budget! The shape of the knife is machine-cut from a sheet of stainless steel, a handle added and the blade sharpened and polished. These knives don't have a bolster, as the blade is attached directly to the handle, so production is a much less complicated process.

Stamped knives aren't as strong or as durable as forged, and the blades tend to be more flexible rather than rigid. Furthermore, they do need sharpening more often, but they will offer quality and value for money, and, for everyday use, will give you good service.

There are 'fors' and 'againsts' for both types of knife, but the deciding factor generally is price. I'd avoid very cheap knives as they won't withstand many years of use, but there are hundreds to choose from in the mid-priced area, all of which will serve you very well for many years. However, I would always say that, if knives are your thing, then spend as much as you can afford, adding one at a time to your collection. This has been my approach, and is how I have now become the proud owner of a very handsome set of knives which are used day in and day out, both at home and when I'm working. They are so good they will probably outlive me and become an heirloom for the future Harradines!

I am now going to take you on a tour of a standard knife so that you understand what each part does.

Let's start at the blade end of the knife, also called the 'point'. The purpose of this point is to pierce and pick up food, but it's also useful for intricate work on fruit and vegetables.

Travelling a little further on, we come to the top part of the blade, called the 'spine'. This is the part of the knife that gives it strength, so it must be fairly thick if you want to cut and chop harder foods, such as butternut squash and turnip.

On a forged knife, just past the spine is the 'bolster', the part between the handle and the blade. This is designed to protect your fingers from the blade edge by giving you a safe place to rest them against whilst cutting. It also helps to balance the knife.

The 'tang' is the steel that extends from the blade or bolster into the handle itself. The best knives have a 'full tang', which means that the steel

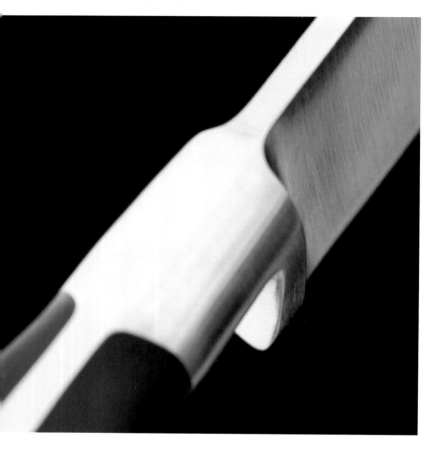

from the blade extends all the way down the length of the handle. This gives the knife strength and durability, and means that it will be robust enough for heavier work in the kitchen.

A 'half tang' means that the steel goes only half way up into the handle. The knife's strength, therefore, particularly for heavier cutting, is not as great as one with a full tang.

The handle is where you hold the knife, obviously, and comes in a variety of materials (mostly wood, plastic or resin), and usually in two pieces – one either side of the tang, then secured using metal rivets.

People often associate weight with quality, but when it comes to knives, this is not always the case: weight is not always king. When I say weight, I mean the overall balance of the knife in your hand. The handle you choose will depend very much on the size of your hand – those with smaller hands tend to prefer lighter handles, whereas someone with larger

you when cutting, place two forefingers under the bolster, the part where the blade meets the handle. Lift the knife and see if it stays there, it should be perfectly balanced. If it isn't, put it down and move on to the next one until you find one that is.

The blade, or I should correctly say the cutting edge of the blade, is the part of the knife that does all the work, so it's important that you consider what you're going to use your knives for before you make your choice. The cutting edge can be smooth, serrated or scalloped, depending on what the knife is to be used for:

- Smooth blades with fine sharp edges are the most common type of kitchen knife, and the blades

slice easily and cleanly through food. They are easy to sharpen using a purpose-built knife sharpener (more about sharpening later).

- Serrated blades have a saw-like appearance to the cutting edge. These serrations help when cutting

hands may prefer something a little heavier. For this reason, it's important to get a feel for the knife in your hand whilst you're in the shop, and before you buy. The knife should feel comfortable in the palm of your hand. If it feels too big or too short, try another size. The end of the handle is usually shaped so it 'flows' downwards in a smooth curve, thus adding to the comfort.

To check the balance of the knife and to ensure that the handle is not so heavy that it will hinder foods that are harder on the outside and softer on the inside, for example, fresh bread. They are also good for sinewy foods, such as meat, which is why steak knives are always serrated. The only downside to this sort of blade is that you won't be able to sharpen it yourself; standard knife sharpeners or butchers' steels will only damage the blade. These knives, therefore, won't be as long-lived as those you can keep sharpening over the years.

• Scalloped or 'indented' blades are usually found on bread knives, but often on Japanese-style knives – the indentations are set into the side of the blade itself and help to stop food sticking to it. They are particularly good on cheese and meat, and raw foods, such as fish.

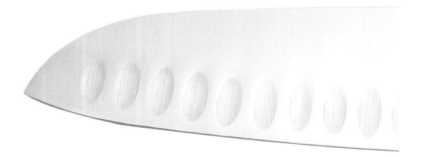

Now, as interesting as this all is, what you really want to know is: "What should I buy?"

If you're starting off a brand new knife collection you need to look for a chef's knife (sometimes referred to as a cook's knife), a paring knife, and a utility knife. These three will form the basis of your knife collection and do the majority of jobs in the kitchen.

• Chef's knife: the most used knife in the kitchen – the blades can be any length from 6 to 14 inches long, but the 8 inch version is a good size to opt for, as it can be used for general slicing, dicing and chopping, and is easily handled.

• Paring knife: a small knife, around 3.5 inches, best used when a chef's knife would be too cumbersome for such tasks as slicing and dicing small fruits and vegetables, or hulling strawberries. 3.5 inches is a good size as you'll be able to do more with it. I even peel potatoes with mine.

• Utility knife: the picture on the next page is deceptive as the utility knife looks exactly the same as the chef's knife. Although longer than a paring knife, it's shorter than a chef's knife, and can be used for cutting medium-sized items. My wife prefers this one, and uses it for pretty much everything because she feels more comfortable with its length and weight.

All these knives have a plain cutting edge and you might ask why there's no serrated blade amongst my top three? The reason is that I believe that if a knife is sharp enough, there really isn't any immediate need for a serrated one. A straight-bladed knife, if sharpened regularly, will do the job just as well. However, there are always exceptions to the rule, and I'll talk a little more about adding to your knife collection in Chapter 10.

You may be tempted to opt for a knife block set, but do check exactly what's in the set, and decide whether you'll actually use each and every knife. If the answer is no, then leave it on the shelf and buy only the knives that you need and will use every day.

You can always buy a separate knife block later. I'll return to the subject of knife storage a little later in the book.

USING A KNIFE

Everyone who has ever used a knife has their own way of cutting, but it is not always the most effective or safest of ways. When we first got together, I watched my left-handed wife chopping away and cringed with fear that was going to slice off her finger. Once I had given her a few pointers on how to hold the knife and use the blade properly, and how to use the other hand to hold what she was cutting

safely, she was soon quite adept at chopping, even for a leftie!

The most important thing to remember is that a sharp knife is a safe knife. If your knife is blunt you'll have to apply a lot of pressure to make the incision, and this is when accidents happen. I check to see if a knife is in need of sharpening by doing the tomato test! Simply take a tomato, place the point of the blade in the skin, and then make a slicing action. If the knife is sharp, it will cut through easily and not tear the skin. If it is blunt, however, it will drag, and you'll end up with a squashed tomato! So, ensuring that your knives are sharpened on a regular basis means

47

A Kitchen Equipped

quickly, more efficiently, and far more safely if you're in control. Shorter knives, such as paring knives, tend to have heavier handles, which give you more control over the blade and the cutting action. After all, you would never use a short knife to carve a joint, or a machete to peel an apple!

I'm sure you've watched cookery programmes where chefs chop at such a speed, their hands are a blur! Of course, expertise like this comes from years of practice, but do remember that they work with them day in, day out, and some chefs do like to show off! Speed isn't important, even if it does look impressive – it's far more important to use a knife properly to slice, dice and chop food into uniform pieces, which means that it will cook more evenly, and ultimately give a better presentation on the plate.

Before you start cutting for real, try and get a feel for the knife: take the knife in your hand so the handle is comfortable in your palm.

Your other hand, known as the 'guiding hand' should be used to hold the food securely when you are cutting it and you need to train this one, too. Potentially, if your fingertips get in the way, you could end up at the emergency department at your local hospital, and this should definitely be avoided! Use a 'claw' action by arching your fingers over the food to hold it in position whilst you're cutting.

Once you have mastered the basic technique of holding your knife properly in one hand, and the claw action of your guiding hand, you are ready to start practicing cutting.

With practice, and by building your confidence in handling knives, you will find it will not take long to learn the art. This will result in you producing more professional results, along with reducing the amount

you'll be able to use them to their full potential, with less chance of harming yourself.

When choosing a knife, make sure it's the right size for the job. You'll complete the task more of injuries and speeding up your preparation time. Not to mention saving you money by not buying gadgets that do the same job as a knife.

CARING FOR YOUR KNIVES
Given that you've spent valuable time choosing your knives, and have spent good money on them, you really want them to last. Treat them kindly and they'll serve you well for many years – use them only as they were made to be used, not as screwdrivers!

The most common ways for knives to get damaged results from the way they are stored, cleaned, and sharpened, but also what type of chopping board you use. So, let's take each of these points and explain how to do it right.

STORAGE
Knives must be stored correctly to avoid personal injury, of course, and to protect the cutting edge. I carry my knives in a professional knife roll, but this wouldn't be very convenient in a domestic kitchen, so I'd suggest any of the following methods:

Storing knives in a drawer
If you store your knives loose in a drawer, not only do you increase the likelihood of cutting yourself (reaching for one whilst, perhaps, distracted by cooking), but also, because the knives can rub against each other, they will blunt more easily and the cutting edge could chip.

If you choose to put your knives in a drawer, use a knife rack. This is usually constructed from wood, has 6-8 slots on two levels, and sits flat in the drawer. The lower slots are for larger knives, such as chefs' and bread knives. The top slots are for shorter knives, such as paring or vegetable knives. By

storing them in this way the knives are stored blade down, so your fingers are safe, and you can easily take the knife of your choice. It also means that your countertop is clear.

More expensive knives often come with protective sleeves, which most people throw away with the packaging, but these are worth hanging on to as they protect the blades (and your fingers) if you do store your knives in a drawer.

but the inner contains hundreds of fibre rods which adapt to hold the knives. You simply push your knives into the rods anywhere you like. The rods themselves can be removed for cleaning, which is excellent from a hygiene point of view.

Storing knives on a magnetic rack

The rack is usually attached to a wall, and a magnetic strip holds the knives. Chefs tend to like these, as they can see which knife is which without having to remove them from a block or drawer, and they are easy to put back after use. You must ensure that the knife is clean, though, as grease on the surface, for example, would mean that the knife might not be as secure as it should be. The only downside to

Storing knives in a block

There are many knife blocks on the market, usually of wooden construction. Storing the block on the worktop means the knives are accessible when you're cooking, but, more importantly, they're stored away safely into their own slots and are in no danger of blunting or chipping. The size of the block, in terms of how many slots you want in it, depends on how many knives you need to house. If you're starting off a knife collection, and perhaps only have the top three we discussed earlier, but you intend to keep adding to them, you might be as well to buy a block which has no pre-cut slots in it. Known as a universal knife block, this is constructed of wood,

this form of storage is that the knives are on show, and accessible to anyone. If you have children, for example, I'd recommend you choose another option, or ensure that the rack is high enough to remain out of their reach.

CLEANING KNIVES

My biggest bugbear where knives are concerned is the dishwasher. Now, don't get me wrong, I think dishwashers are fantastic in many ways, certainly from a deep cleaning point of view, but cleaning knives in this way can cause them to blunt very quickly, and the salts from the dishwasher can, over time, eat into the blade. No steel is yet invented is completely 'stainless'! You'll also find that, even though they've been through the drying cycle,

Diswasher Safe

there are often water marks on the blades, even rust spots, which you have to clean off anyway. Additionally, the heat from the washer can loosen the handles, and, in some cases, crack them, so it really is best to hand wash if you want to keep them at their best.

In my opinion, even if the manufacturers say a knife is dishwasher-proof, I would always recommend that you wash it in warm soapy water, dry it immediately, and put it away.

Just a word of warning: When washing them, never put your sharp knives into a sink full of soapy water – you could very easily cut yourself whilst fishing around in there with your hands. Instead, leave them on the side, and wash them one by one.

SHARPENING YOUR KNIVES

You don't have to sharpen your knives daily or even weekly to keep them in tip top condition. Every two weeks should be enough, or whenever you feel that the blade isn't cutting as well as it should (if you're not sure, do the tomato test!)

In the good old days we always used a butcher's steel, which, although very effective, was very tricky to use if you weren't skilled in using it. It's imperative that the steel is positioned to the knife blade at a

specific angle – get this wrong and you'll spoil the blade edge and blunt the knife.

Nowadays, there are many are easy to use domestic knife sharpeners on the market, where you simply slide the knife in between the steel mechanism inside five or six times to get perfectly sharpened knives without the hassle.

Sharpeners with rotating steel rollers within the mechanism are, in my opinion, the best for domestic use, as they move with the blade as the knife is being pulled through with no sharding of the blade. Some less expensive sharpeners can be a little 'over keen', and you'll see tiny fragments of steel come off the knife as you sharpen (not good). Spending a little extra on a good knife sharpener really is worth it.

CHOPPING BOARDS

Knife blades will blunt very quickly if used on very hard surfaces, such as ceramic, glass or marble. I would always recommend either wood or plastic boards.

Wood is the kindness material to the cutting edge of a knife as, being a natural material, it doesn't blunt the blade as quickly. Plastic is the next best thing, although it will blunt knives faster than wood, but the advantage is the lower cost compared to wood, plus you can put it in the dishwasher.

There are plenty to choose from, and they come in all shapes and sizes, but I'd suggest you go for a small one for chopping herbs, lemons (for your gin and tonics), etc., and a larger one for vegetables, meat, etc.

Hygiene is paramount with chopping boards – they must be cleaned very thoroughly as they can harbour germs. Wooden boards are very hygienic as the wood itself has its own built in defence mechanism, but it still needs a good scrub after use! Most good quality wooden boards are sealed with a non-toxic protective layer to help keep their appearance but, more importantly, to prevent absorption of water when washed.

The best way to clean a wooden board is to simply wipe over the surface with a damp cloth, or wash in warm soapy water, then dry it off. Don't soak a wooden board, as this will cause the wood to warp in time. You can go one step further and, every month or so, rub some olive oil into the board to prevent it from drying out.

If wood is not your thing, choose a plastic board (ideally a non-porous, non-absorbent item, to ensure that no germs can linger on the surface of the board or in grooves that develop on the cutting surface). Wash it in the sink with hot soapy water, or pop it in the dishwasher.

Having different coloured boards for different foods is commonplace in the catering industry, and this idea is also becoming more popular in the domestic kitchen. A great benefit of having various colours is to avoid cross-contamination, such as with the mixing of raw and cooked meats, although all boards should be washed thoroughly between each use.

So, if you're cutting raw meat you would use a red board, use blue for raw fish, yellow for cooked meat, green for salad and fruit, brown for vegetables, and white for bakery and dairy. You can even buy a rack to store them all if your kitchen space will allow it.

Of course, you might not eat all these different foods, so to be realistic, opt for just two or three if that's all you need. In our kitchen we use a red board for all raw meats, a green board for salads and fruit, and a white board for everything else, and this works well for us.

That brings us to the end of our chapter on knives and accessories. The message is clear: your knives are an investment so choose wisely, store well, treat with care and sharpen regularly, and your knives will give you a lifetime of good use.

Kitchen utensils

When you walk into a cook shop you are faced with a massive selection of kitchen tools and utensils, all made of different materials, in different sizes and shapes, and for many uses. To be honest, there will be many than can be replaced with a knife (we've covered that bit!) but they are oh so enticing, and you could be tempted to buy – so read on!

I for one admit that I used to be a bit of a gadget freak, and my wife despaired when I would come home with the latest piece of equipment that had caught my eye. However, I quickly learned my lesson, discovering that after it was used a few times, the novelty wore off and it was relegated to the back of the drawer; yes, I admit it Mrs Harradine!

The key is to think about what you will use on a day-to-day basis, and how that utensil could be used in several ways. Do that now and you will save yourself from a drawer full of stuff that just gathers dust.

The list coming up comprises the basics we all need in our kitchens, many of them are multi-use. However, there may also be specific items that you will require. For example, if you regularly bake, you may need a piping set or pastry cutters – just add these to your own personal list of must-haves.

So, let's talk about the definitive 'must-have' kitchen utensils ...

- Slotted turner

- Three wooden spoons in various sizes

- A pair of silicon tongs

- Spaghetti spoon

- Large serving spoon

- Large draining spoon

- Silicone spatula

- Two sizes of balloon hand whisks, small and large

- Medium-sized colander

- Medium-sized sieve

- A set of mixing bowls

- Potato peeler

- A good quality can opener

- Box grater with various cutter sizes

- Potato ricer

- Silicone splatter guard without handle

- Silicone headed pastry brush

- Silicone rolling pin

- A set of measuring jugs and spoons

- A wire cooling rack

- Silicone oven mitts

- Salt and pepper mills

- A jam thermometer if you are a jam maker or enjoy making chocolate

- Kitchen scales

You will find all these items and more, available in stainless steel, plastic, nylon and silicone, but if you have opted for non-stick cookware then it's best to avoid the stainless steel versions as they can scratch the surface over time.

I have to say that I am not a great advocate of plastic and nylon utensils, as I've had too many melt and shrivel when inadvertently left in a pan or when they've come into contact with hot fat; not good when cooking eggs!

Silicone is my most favoured material, as it can withstand heat up to 250°C, is very flexible, non-slip (important if you have dexterity issues), and is easy to clean and dishwasher-safe.

Whatever material you opt for, always try to buy one-piece items, and by that I mean there is no separate handle attached to the head, rather, the whole thing is made from one single piece. Items which have separate handles tend to work loose in time, and you end up having to replace them, so buy wise to start with.

Slotted turners

The most used utensil in the kitchen as you will be using it to fry eggs, to lift food out of baking trays

and grill pans, and to remove cooked fish from dishes or steamers. I would suggest that, when choosing one, it needs to be flat and not too thick at the lifting end as this would make it awkward to get under delicate foods. The slots allow liquids and fats to drain away.

Wooden spoons

Whenever I see a wooden spoon, it always reminds me of when I used to watch my Granny cooking, as they were then – and still are – a staple item in the kitchen. They are suitable to use in every sort of pan, clean easily, are robust, and are cheap to buy. Every kitchen should have a set.

Tongs

These are very versatile and can do a variety of jobs, from turning meat in pans or under the grill, to lifting delicate asparagus from the steamer. Great

when barbecuing, too. Buy those with slightly longer handles, and either made totally from silicone or with a silicone inlay as this makes them safer to use and grip.

Spoons

In general, everyday cooking, there's always a need for spoons, as these can be used for a multitude of things. Size-wise, I'd go for quite a large capacity, about the size of four tablespoons is good as you can use this for anything from dishing up a casserole to spooning out the vegetables.

Spaghetti spoons are great little things as they lift, separate, and drain the pasta as you take it from the pan or colander. I also use mine for draining small vegetables, such as peas, without having to use a colander at all (less washing up!).

Silicone spatula

My wife says that this is her favourite piece of equipment in the kitchen. The spatula is shaped flat on the top and curved at the bottom which allows it to easily bend to get into corners of pans and bowls, brilliant if you're making cakes as you can get out the last bit of the mixture, so there's no waste. They are also fantastic when making mashed potatoes – after you have mashed them (or put them through the ricer, more about that shortly), add the butter and milk and use the spatula to mix them all together to get it smooth and creamy.

Balloon whisks

These are so useful. You can use them when making gravy, sauces, soups, or just for whipping up cream. I would recommend buying two sizes, a small one and a large one, as these will cover most eventualities.

Sieve
Plastic or metal mesh items do the job equally well, although the metal versions are stronger and will last for longer. I'd suggest a medium size, as this will serve you well for sieving flour, icing sugar, straining sauces, etc.

Mixing bowls
Whether you're mixing the ingredients for an omelette, making custard, or just mixing ingredients

Colander
Go for a medium-sized colander as this can be used for everything that needs draining, from small quantities of peas, to a pan full of potatoes or pasta. It can also be used when preparing vegetables, as you can rinse them off and drain them thoroughly before cooking. They are available in a variety of materials, all of which do the job equally well. You can even buy foldup colanders, made from silicone, which fit easily into a drawer – great for mobile homes where space is short.

for a marinade, you will always need a bowl. I'd recommend a set of three – small, medium and large – so that you can choose one according to what you're mixing.

You may find that bowls which have a helper handle at one side very useful for holding the bowl steady, especially if you're whisking or mixing large quantities. Many come with a non-stick silicone ring on the bottom to stop the bowl slipping away whilst in use. Go for those with a pouring lip at one side; less mess when you're filling pastry cases, bun tins, etc.

Bowls come in a variety of materials, from plastic to silicone and ceramic, but they all do the same job. If you want to double up and save yourself a bit of money, you could use plastic food storage containers (see Chapter 9) as a mixing bowl.

Potato peeler

I've tried many peelers in my lifetime and the best ones by far are those shaped like a 'Y', which means whether you are left- or right-handed, they are easy to use. Unlike the single-sided swivel peelers, Y-shaped ones tend to have a more robust handle, so are more comfortable in your hand – and, if you have dexterity problems, it gives you more control as less grip is required.

Some can be very sharp so do take care to keep your fingers out of the way, try holding the vegetable in the palm of your hand and slice downwards. Some have an eye remover on them, too, which is worth having, particularly for potatoes.

Can openers

Back in the good old days we had the old fashioned can openers, where you stuck the sharp end in and wiggled it around the edge of the can until the top came off, then promptly cut yourself on the jagged edge! Once manufacturers had realised these were not the safest things in the kitchen, we moved on to what is still available, the 'butterfly' can opener.

These work perfectly well and are as cheap as chips, but you do have to grip them very hard to get them to work; not good if you have limited hand strength. Plus, you still get the jagged can lid at the end of it.

By far the most effective and safest of all can openers are the more modern versions which have large comfortable handles. Minimal pressure is required to attach it to the can, and they have a large turning knob to turn the opener easily. Most of these leave a smooth edge on the can lid, so there's less likelihood of you cutting yourself when removing it from the opener itself.

Graters

Everyone will need to grate some cheese at some point, but we use them for so much more nowadays. You can just buy a simple one-sided grater for your cheese if that's all you need it for, but otherwise it's far more cost effective to buy a box grater which has as many as three or four different grating sides to it, for fine, medium, and coarse grating and slicing.

So, not only can you grate cheese, you can also grate nutmeg or ginger, for example, or slice cabbage and carrots for a coleslaw, and then take the zest off a lemon. So many uses in one item, and fewer gadgets cluttering up your cupboards and drawers.

Because it sits flat on a work surface, you can use one hand to secure the grater in place, and use the other to do the grating without too much effort (perfect for those with limited hand strength).

Potato ricer

The usual way to mash your potatoes is to use a masher, but let's face it, it's hard work, particularly if you have a large pan to get through, and you always end up with some lumps in the mash, no matter how hard you try!

Although it means a bit of extra washing up, this is the one gadget you really should consider adding to your collection. You can use it not only for your potatoes, but any fruit or vegetables that you want to puree.

The potatoes go into the ricer, you press down on the handle, and the potatoes come through the other end in 'strands', a bit like meat through a mincer.

Check that the holes in the ricer bottom are a good size, not too small, as otherwise you have to cook your potatoes or hard vegetables, such as swede or turnip, until they are very soft to force them through.

A great bit of kit, and, once you've used one, you'll never moan about having to wash it up as your mash will be just like you see chefs making on the telly – I think they call it Pomme Puree!

Splatter guard

If you're frying anything in oil that spits the moment you increase the heat, the splatter guard is invaluable. It stops splashes and keeps your hob top clean. If you buy a silicone version, with either a fold up handle or no handle at all, you can use it in the microwave to stop things spattering when cooking (check the manufacturer's instructions before using to be on the safe side). I wouldn't be without mine.

Silicone pastry brush

These silicone versions are far better than the old fashioned bristled brushes, as they don't clog up and are much easier to clean (and are, therefore, more hygienic). Great when you need to egg wash the tops of pies, or simply brush oil over meat or chicken ready for the oven. If you're watching your cholesterol intake, simply put a tiny amount of oil into your frying pan and use the brush to coat the entire bottom of the pan. You will find plenty of uses for this little utensil.

Silicone rolling pin

Whilst it is rarer than hens' teeth to see Mel, my wife of some years, use such an implement (apart from brandishing it at me!), if you do like to cook, then at some point you will need to roll out some pastry, or perhaps crush biscuits for a cheesecake base, or tenderize some meats. So a rolling pin is a must.

Walk into a cookshop and you will be met by ceramic, marble, plastic and wooden versions, but in my opinion by far the most effective is one made with a silicone outer. I'll be talking more about the wonders of silicone in Chapter 6, but for now all you need to know is that the non-stick properties make rolling out pastry an absolute doddle, and you'll need to use little or no flour on the pin, and the pastry won't stick to it or tear as you roll. Perfect results every time.

Measuring jugs & spoons

We have all played a guessing game when it comes to baking and cooking, but often recipes can go badly wrong if you've used the wrong quantities just because you didn't have the right piece of equipment. I am as guilty as anyone of this misdemeanor! However, by spending just a couple of pounds, you could buy a set of measuring jugs and spoons, and/or measuring cups, and get great results every time you cook.

I'd suggest you buy a set of plastic jugs, small, medium and large, that sit one inside the other when not in use. Ensure they have both metric and imperial measurements on either side, as older cookery books will only have the imperial weights shown. You can buy glass measuring jugs but they are more difficult to stack and store in your cupboards, and, to be honest, plastic does just as well, and is a lot cheaper.

Measuring spoons and cups are used for small quantities. You'll usually find a selection of different sizes which sit inside one another when not in use, all housed together on a ring. Spoons and cups can be used with liquids or dry ingredients, and are available in imperial and metric measurements.

Wire cooling rack

If you have a grill pan with an existing wire rack you won't need to buy anything else as this will double up as a cooling rack. Racks are usually metal, sometimes non-stick coated, and can be easily stored when not in use. If you are a baker and need to cool cakes and buns, etc., a foldaway, tiered wire rack may be useful as, not only do you get the cooling space needed, it also takes up only a small amount of space on your counter top. They do not

cost a great deal but are handy little items in the kitchen.

Silicone oven mitts

We've all used a tea towel to get food out of the oven, etc., and we've all managed to burn ourselves in the process! Fabric oven gloves and mitts are all very well, but they tend to wear very quickly, burn easily, and before you know it, you're replacing them with another set. My recommendation would be to go for a pair of silicone mitts, as you can handle things up to 250°C, so there's no worry about them melting! I'd also suggest that you buy the ones that come further up your arm, covering the wrist in particular as this is the bit we always end up catching when we reach into the oven. From a safety point of view, silicone is non-slip, so there's less chance of accidents when lifting and carrying hot trays, pans, etc.

Salt & pepper mills

I'm sure that there are thousands upon thousands of homes across the world that have old wooden salt and pepper mills that are lying dormant, perhaps because they never worked properly in the first place, or are still being used in a vain attempt to get a wee morsel of ground salt onto the food!

Salt is extremely corrosive, and can cause a spindle and steel type salt mill to give up the ghost rather quickly, which is often the reason why we end up reverting to the old fashioned salt and pepper pots!

My advice here is simple – simply walk into a cook shop and ask the assistant for ceramic salt and pepper mills. Why? Because ceramic is one of the toughest materials known to man, and it will grind

because people tend to forget that if they make jams or chocolate, or do a bit of sugar spinning now and again, then a thermometer is absolutely essential to get perfect results. A general, traditionally-designed cooking thermometer is fine for all these uses; it doesn't have to be specifically designed for any one.

However, if you want to go to the next level, there are digital versions available, but they do the same thing and are often more expensive. Why pay more when you don't have to, is my philosophy!

And finally ... kitchen scales

Are scales a necessity in the kitchen? If you are baking, or following recipes correctly, then, in my opinion the answer is a definite 'yes'. In general cooking, I usually go with taste and smell, but baking is a 'measured science', and if you want that cake to come out perfectly then you need to follow your recipe ingredient weights – to the gram (or ounce)!

In the USA they measure in cup sizes, and use measuring spoons for smaller ingredients (a much more simple way of baking), but as all European cookbooks work in metric units, a set of scales is necessary.

Scales have been used by cooks for hundreds of years. Originally called 'balance scales', and simple to use, these scales have a balance arm with an oval-shaped dish at one side and a weighing plate at the other where you place the different-sized weights (marked in either metric or imperial). Just place the weight you require on one side, then fill the bowl until the scales balance. The only disadvantage is that they are heavy and take up space in the kitchen. My mum is still using her antique balance scales which have been passed down from generation

salt and pepper forever and a day, long enough for you to pass them on as an heirloom! Every time you use them you will thank me for this bit of advice, as these are something that we all use to season our food, day in, day out. There's nothing quite like freshly milled peppercorns or sea salt to add flavour to your food, so it really is worth buying good quality versions.

Jam thermometer

I have added this to the list of 'must-haves' only

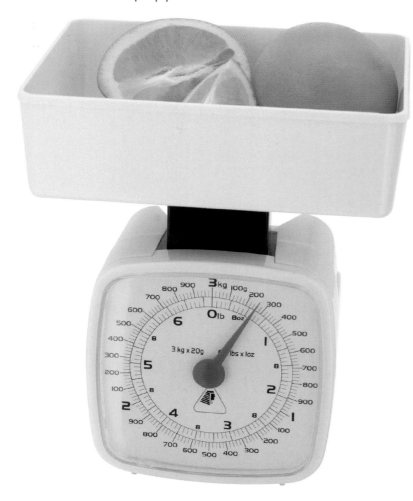

like face with a dial and pointer and a jug or bowl where you place your ingredients resting on top of a weighing plate. As you add to the jug or bowl, this pushes down on the weighing plate and the weight is registered on the 'clock' face. Most of these scales have dual grams and imperial measurements. They are much cheaper than the balance and electronic types, and are lighter so you can easily move them around the kitchen. Usually the jug or bowl can be inverted and placed over the dial area thus taking up less space in your cupboard.

My personal favourite is the electronic or digital scale. Back in the late 1980s, I worked as Sales and Marketing Director for Waymaster Ltd, a major UK scales company based in Reading with a history going back to the 1940s. The company was a master in the design and manufacture of kitchen scales, and was responsible for designing the first flat battery-operated electronic unit. I feel privileged to have seen first hand how this sector of the scale market came to fruition, right from the embryonic stages of the first design drawings to seeing it on the shelves in stores. So as you can imagine, I am a bit passionate about my kitchen scales!

Of course, other manufacturers soon got in on the act, and nowadays there are hundreds of electronic scales to choose from, so there's little wonder that customers become so confused when they see such a vast array laid before them in cookshops. Which one to choose?

The key thing to remember is if you want precision and absolute accuracy, electronic or digital scales are the ones for you. They are so precise you can weigh just a few specks of sugar!

They are battery operated, with touch controls so all you do is press the on/off button and an

to generation, and even now they're in perfect condition.

Another type of scale that has been around for many a year is the 'Add and Weigh' scales, available in plastic or metal construction or a combination of both. They are available in all shapes and sizes, but work basically in the same way. They have a clock-

68

The author using a kitchen gadget at an in-store demonstration.

electronic LCD screen greets you. Choose between imperial or metric with just a touch of a button, depending on your recipe.

Most of these type of scales incorporate an 'add and weigh' facility, which basically means that you can weigh all the ingredients for a cake mixture all at once in the same bowl. How? Just pop your chosen mixing bowl onto the scale, press a button and the weight of the bowl disappears and goes to a zero. Now you can start to add the ingredients – for example, pour in 175g sugar and then press the add and weight button and again, the weight goes back to zero. Then add 175g butter, press the button and, voila! It goes back to zero.

Beat the sugar and butter together, add the eggs, then place the bowl back onto the scales, zero the weight again, then sift the flour into the bowl until the scale reaches the magic 175g again. Remove the bowl from the scale, and continue making the cake. Easy!

Not only are these scales light, they are very slim, so are easily stored in a kitchen drawer, and cleaning is a breeze; just wipe the weighing plate with a damp cloth.

These scales retail for around £40- £50, and it will be money well spent as they will give you years of use, and, more importantly, give you perfect results when you're baking and cooking. You certainly can't blame the scales when your cake ends up as a disaster!

Once you have these basics, you'll have exactly what you will need for day-to-day use – no unnecessary clutter in cupboards and drawers – and, as time goes by, you'll have space available to add to your collection.

Before you go out there buying additional items that you think you might need next, flick to the very last chapter of this book for a list of others items that you may want to buy, in 'Adding to my kitchen collection'!

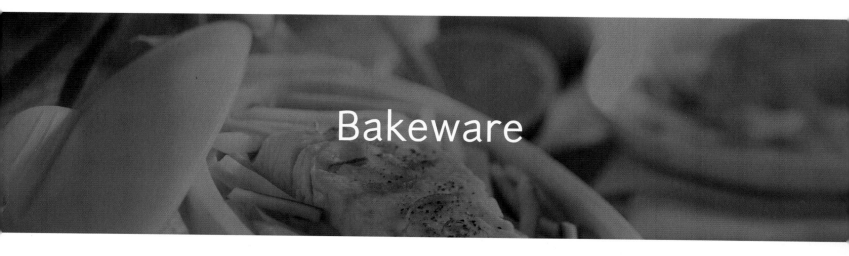

Bakeware

Whether you are a regular baker or some-time cook, everyone needs baking sheets, roasting dishes, and bun trays in their kitchen. These all come under the 'bakeware' umbrella, but can be used for much more than just 'baking'.

Step into High Street or online cookware shops and you'll be bombarded with a huge array of products, all vying for your attention, and all looking extremely tempting. However, like I keep saying, not everything that you see and like will be of any use to you when you get it home. Remember your budget, and buy only those items you know will be taken out of the cupboard at least two or three times a week – to use that is, not just to dust!

My wife proved the point not so long ago. Never having been one for baking (or cooking, if the truth be known!), she came in from a day's shopping trip with ... wait for it ... a springform cake tin! Now, this isn't generally the top thing of her list when she goes shopping, and so, when I'd stopped laughing,

I asked her why she had bought it (bearing in mind the lack of baking she does). She calmly stated that she thought it would come in "... handy". For what I'm not sure, but without a shadow of doubt, at that moment she proved my point that impulse purchases are not always good.

If you're wondering about the fate of the cake tin, well, after she decided that it wasn't much good as a helmet or for using as a plant pot, she passed it to me for use as ... a cake tin. Strange that.

Anyway, enough reminiscing, let's get on with talking about bakeware.

There are many materials used to make bakeware, but the most common are aluminium, usually non-stick coated and also known as metalware, and one of the most innovative materials known to man ... silicone.

I use metal and silicone on a daily basis, but tend to veer towards silicone as I am a great fan. So much so, I have dedicated a whole chapter to it, so I would

highly recommend that you read it before you make your decision as to which bakeware to buy.

However, just for now, I want to talk about the difference between these two materials, and the pros and cons for both.

ALUMINIUM BAKEWARE, OR 'METALWARE'

Whether lined in non-stick or not, aluminium is one of the best materials for bakeware; it's lightweight and conducts heat very quickly. This results in even cooking, very important whether you're baking a cake or cooking oven chips.

Plain aluminium without any non-stick coating tends to be used in the catering industry, but you do have to know what you're doing to avoid burning or sticking. If baking, tins have to be lined with greaseproof paper, or greased quite heavily, and this type requires particular care in seasoning before and after use. So, from a convenience point of view, in a domestic kitchen this can often be a bugbear.

Most people tend to opt for aluminium with a non-stick lining. This allows the same even cooking, but with the added advantage of quick food release and easy cleaning.

However, if you're baking cakes, you'll need to line the tin with greaseproof paper, or heavily grease it, as a certain amount of sticking will occur. If you're using the tin to cook a joint of meat, for example, the fats from the meat will do the job for you.

As I mentioned earlier (in the cookware chapter of this book), there are different grades of non-stick coating, and you'll see many price points when out and about in the stores. As a rule, the cheaper the bakeware, the lighter the aluminium, and the thinner

(though not in the microwave or on the hob top, as it doesn't usually have an appropriate base). However, you can get roasting tins with a proper sandwich base, so that you can roast the meat in the oven, and then use the juices to make gravy on the hob top. If this is something that you like to do regularly, then this is the type of roasting tin you will need.

Cleaning is best done by hand rather than in the dishwasher, as the salts in the machine will erode the non-stick coating.

My recommendation, therefore, would be, if metalware is your choice, ensure it has some weight to it, the non-stick is a good one, and it has some sort of guarantee. The packaging will tell you this.

SILICONE

Good quality silicone does exactly the same job as metal bakeware but with added advantages in that it is very versatile and can be used in the oven, microwave, freezer, and fridge, is very easy to clean, being a natural non-stick, and is dishwasher-safe. However, you cannot use it on the hob top or under a grill.

It requires very little greasing, and you don't have to line the cake moulds when baking, as the cake will come out with only a little flexing of the mould.

Silicone doesn't stain or retain odours after cooking, and cleaning is an absolute doddle as nothing sticks – wash it by hand in warm soapy water or put it in the dishwasher.

The main comment from the general public is that they cannot get over how they can put it in the oven when it is so soft – it's floppy for goodness sake! They simply cannot believe that it can perform exactly the same function as metal bakeware. That

the non-stick lining. If you're going to use it only now and again, then this is fine, perhaps in a holiday home or caravan, for example, but if you want it to last for many years then you should opt for a heavier gauge of aluminium and a renowned non-stick lining. Pay a little more and the tin will not warp when put into a hot oven, and the non-stick coating will remain in place even with a lot of use. As I keep saying, you get what you pay for!

Take care not to use stainless steel or metal utensils on the non-stick lining, though, as it will become scratched and cause the lining to bubble and peel off in time.

You can use aluminium bakeware in the oven and under the grill, and it can also go in the freezer

is until they watch me take a beautifully baked cake out of the oven and see me literally peel the cake mould away with no sticking and no greaseproof lining! Well, they say seeing is believing!

From a storage point of view, you can bend and fold it. When I demonstrate it in stores, I always have an empty receptacle on hand and show how it can be stored by forcing it in, making it go completely out of shape, leave it for five or ten minutes and then pull it back out and ... voila! The mould goes straight back to its original shape! This is great stuff if storage space is an issue, as you can roll two or three items together and put an elastic band around them before popping them in a drawer – something that you cannot do with metalware!

Ultimately, whether you want to bake a cake, roast a Sunday joint, make biscuits, or simply cook fish fingers, every kitchen needs a good selection of bakeware to do all these jobs.

Which option you go for is purely personal choice – metal bakeware has been tried and tested for many years, whilst silicone is relatively new in comparison, but try not to be blinkered into thinking one is better than the other – they both have outstanding benefits, it's just finding the ones that suits you and your type of cooking.

So, let's talk about what shapes you need to fulfill your everyday needs ... but bear in mind the size of your oven, as larger bakeware items may not fit in!

• A large roaster – to be used for roasting the Sunday joint or chicken, making a large pie or lasagne, roasting potatoes, or general oven use.

You can use a silicone mould for heavier foods such as a joint, but may feel it's too flexible and prefer something more solid to hold it. In this case you could either opt for a metal roaster, or place the silicone roaster on a metal or reinforced silicone baking tray.

• A square cake pan – big enough to do smaller pieces of meat, vegetables, oven chips, etc., but also useful if you want to make a square cake.

• A 12-hole bun or muffin mould – essential for making cakes, buns and the like, but can also double up to make Yorkshire puddings.

• A shallow baking tray – for making biscuits, cookies, swiss rolls, roulades, or simply to cook pork chops and roasted veggies.

- Two round cake moulds, around eight inches in diameter – perfect for making sponge cakes, or if you just want to roast a small piece of meat. These will fit into most microwaves if you opt for the silicone version.

There is just one more section that we need to talk about as this does fall into the bakeware category.

OVEN-TO-TABLEWARE

Every kitchen needs a small selection of dishes that can be used in the oven to roast or bake, but which looks good enough to be taken straight to the table. After all, no-one wants to see a boring grey baking tin on their dinner table!

Although you can use them purely as serving dishes, to get the most from them and get your money's worth, you should give them a dual use, and make the most of their features by using them in the oven and under the grill. In some cases, you can even put them into the microwave, too.

There are three basic materials used for this type of oven-to-table bakeware: stone, ceramic and enamelled cast iron.

Stone

When I was a lad, I can clearly remember my Granny cooking with stone dishes in her coal fired oven; but they were always very discoloured and looked very well worn – when questioned she said that it was due to all the goodness that had soaked into them over years of use. Of course, she was absolutely right: they might have looked as if several generations had used them but they certainly did a fantastic job of holding the heat and cooking the food beautifully. I guess they were the precursor to what we see in cook shops today.

Basic stone bakeware has no coatings either inside or out. To build up its resistance to sticking, it does needs seasoning with oil regularly, and it is best washed up with just plain warm water, using little or no detergents to clean it as this will just remove its natural non-stick built up over use. If anything does stick to it, it can be easily scraped off using a silicone spatula, then run it under hot water, air dry and store in your oven, as this will keep the stone in tip top condition.

Take care not to expose stoneware to very extreme temperatures, for example taking a very hot dish that has been in the oven and then plunge it into cold water, as it is prone to thermal shock and will crack. Instead, allow the dish to cool thoroughly and then wash it.

Stone bakeware might look ancient with just a few months of use, but in this case, it really is age before beauty!

Ceramic

Ceramic is one of the most popular types of oven-to-tableware, and you'll find a huge range, in bright colours and varying shapes and sizes, in most stores. They are relatively inexpensive so you can probably afford to buy a few pieces to compliment your bakeware collection.

The best thing about ceramic dishes is that they have a vitreous enamel finish to them, making them very easy to clean. They can be used in the oven and under the grill, with many also being microwave, freezer and dishwasher-proof – just check the manufacturer's directions first.

Enamelled cast iron

If you want to go for the crème de la crème, then you can do no better than enamelled cast iron bakeware dishes, as they hold the heat like no others, and are perfect if you cook in an Aga oven or at high temperatures. Like ceramic bakeware, the cast iron is coated in a coloured enamel on the outside, and a vitreous enamel on the inside, to give a non-stick lining.

One downside is that it tends to be much more expensive due to the lengthy and costly manufacturing process, another is that it's heavy. If lifting is difficult for anyone in your family, you do need to look for a lighter option.

So, that brings us to the end of our bakeware section. Having been given all the various options, the important thing is that you buy what you feel comfortable with, and that you're happy with your purchase. You may do as we do, and use a combination of all and have the best of both worlds. Read on for more information on the wonders of silicone! Then the decision is yours!

The wonders of silicone

Traditionally, metal bakeware has for many years been the favoured material, and my mother-in-law still has baking trays that she had when she first got married some 50-odd years ago.

So, to suggest moving away from the tried-and-tested to something completely alien is often met with reluctance, as it means getting your mind around the fact that this silicone is NOT going to melt in the oven, and it WILL bake your cakes beautifully.

My love affair with silicone began back in the late 1990s when I was a guest presenter on a well known TV shopping channel. At that time, this type of material was mostly unheard of, particularly in the kitchen equipment world, but the viewers that day must have thought I put up a convincing argument for having it, as I sold out of several thousand cake moulds in a 20 minute session. I think the powers that be at the shopping channel must have thought it was a fluke, though, so put me on air again with it a week or two later to test

the water. Result! A complete sell out this time, and so silicone became a very regular product on the channel, and I earned myself a nickname – Mr Silicone – as most of the products I was selling on air at that time had some silicone either in or on them somewhere! So, what I'm trying to explain really is that silicone is not a new-fangled thing, it has been around for many years, and those TV viewers who bought it are testament to that. It must have been memorable as my nickname stuck, and is still used to this day!

In my experience, people are hesitant about buying silicone, largely because they don't understand it; where it comes from, and about its outstanding natural benefits, and, more importantly, how to use it. I will try to explain …

WHAT IS SILICONE?

Everyone thinks that silicone is a new invention, but it was actually discovered back in the 18th century, when it was known as silicate. Silicone is actually one of the most abundantly natural elements on Earth, and exists in common sand and rock, and forms part of our everyday lives if you did but know it! Glass, pottery, concrete, and even the bricks of your house are made from silicates, so you're already surrounded by it!

Back in the 1980s, some clever scientists found that 100% silicone in its solid form has many natural characteristics. It was found to have unique qualities for pliability, durability, heat resistance at extreme temperatures (both high and low), is odourless, and does not transfer smells.

Perfect for cookware! And so silicone for use in the kitchen was born.

One of the main questions I get asked is: "Is it safe?" I would say wholeheartedly, "Yes". It is absolutely astounding the lengths manufacturers have to go to in order to obtain certification in the housewares industry. Their products must conform to stringent regulations, and silicone bakeware must be made of FDA-approved food grade silicone – this is always made clear on the packaging – so that it is perfectly safe for human use.

So why is it so good in the kitchen?

Silicone is an invaluable invention for it has so many advantages over the other cookware and bakeware available on the market:

• It is naturally non-stick, excellent for the quick release of foods, and easy to clean.

• It's odourless, goes not give off fumes, and there is no transfer of taste from cooking one sort of food to another, so you can bake a cake in it one day and use it for roast potatoes the next.

• It's extremely flexible, and has an in-built 'shape memory' – if you bend, fold, roll and just squash silicone, when released, even after long periods, it just springs back into its original shape without any detriment at all. This makes is very easy to store – recent introductions have been the collapsible mixing bowl and steam case, both of which fold flat.

• It's heat resistant up to 220°C-250°C, and can be used in the freezer to -40°C, so you can cook something in a mould, then cover it and put it straight in the freezer – and even when frozen solid, the silicone mould literally pulls away from the food within it.

How do you use silicone bakeware?

For the bakers amongst you, you probably will have always used metal cake tins, but don't be fooled into thinking that this is your only option – silicone bakeware cooks as evenly as metal, and has the added advantage that, rather than having to run a knife around the edge of the baked cake whilst still in the tin, due to its flexibility, you can literally peel the silicone mould away from the cake with nothing sticking or being left on the mould.

Initially, for the first couple of uses, I would suggest that you lightly grease the mould before putting your cake mixture in – this is just to 'season' the mould, like you would do with metal bakeware – but there's no need to line it with greaseproof paper.

After a few uses, the surface of the silicone takes on an excellent non-stick property, which means you can do away with lightly oiling it in the certainty that your cakes will not stick and you get perfect results every time.

Many customers in the past commented on how the moulds felt 'flimsy', and so they felt they needed to use a baking tray, either silicone or metal, under the mould to get it in and out of the oven. The manufacturers have listened to their customers and most good quality silicone is now made with reinforced sides and rims to give more stability.

Of course, you can still use a support underneath if you like – as you must feel comfortable with it – so use the tray if you prefer, but rest assured, the silicone will still do its job even so.

Unlike metal bakeware which holds the heat for a good while once it comes out of the oven, silicone quickly cools – in fact, within only a minute or two, it is cool to the touch. This isn't to say that the food is cooling as rapidly, that will still be very hot so

- You can use it in the oven, microwave, fridge or freezer, and it's dishwashersafe.

- It has a non-corrosive resistant surface, so there's no non-stick surface to bubble, peel or rust.

- It is extremely light, so it's perfect if you have limited lifting ability or if you want to use it in your holiday home/caravan.

- In a nutshell, it is indestructible, unless you throw it on the fire or cut it with scissors or a knife!

don't poke your finger in it! And you should always use oven gloves when taking it out of the oven or microwave.

I do many kids cookery classes and I always use silicone for reasons of safety, and it's certainly something to consider if you have children who enjoy getting into the kitchen.

If you or anyone in your family has dexterity problems, I would absolutely advise using silicone because it's very light, easy to manipulate, and, as discussed earlier, it cools so quickly there's no danger of burning your hands.

What should you look for when buying silicone? There are many makes of silicone on the market, some better than others. I'd recommend that you look closely at the packaging to establish that the product is 100% silicone, as poorer quality silicone can give off odours and can burn away. Sub-standard silicone will most definitely affect the overall performance, and you'll be disappointed with the results – plus you'll think I have been telling porky pies!

Price is always a good indicator of quality. I've heard customers complain that they've bought a mould (and it was only £5 for the set!), but then said it was rubbish and that they would never buy silicone again; once bitten, twice shy. Once consumers lose confidence in something, they will always steer clear of it, and go back to what they've always used.

This is a real shame, though, as, if you invest wisely in your silicone pieces and buy good quality, I can assure you, you will NOT be disappointed.

An example of this was with my lovely mother-in-law, a Yorkshire girl through-and-through and an expert at making THE best Yorkshire puddings in the world. She's the one who still has the baking trays given to her as a wedding present, and, up until this point, had always used metal bakeware to cook her puddings. So, when I gave her a silicone 12-hole bun sheet to use, she looked me straight in the eye and announced that there was no way that it would work. The lard wouldn't melt and get smoking blue as it does in metal bakeware, so the puddings wouldn't rise, and they would be as flat as flounders! Plus, she confidently informed me, the bakeware adds to the flavour, so they would definitely not taste the same as when she does them in her old tins. And so the gauntlet was thrown down!

She was desperate to prove me wrong, but I knew better, having tried and tested the theory for many a year. So, off she went, made her usual mixture (not sure of the quantities, it's a secret recipe handed down from mother to daughter over many generations), put her little blob of lard into each bun hole and, sure enough, we got the blue smoke indicating it was time to put the pudding mixture in.

Once back in the oven, she folded her arms, looked me again in the eye and said, "It will never work", although I think she was secretly surprised that even the lard had done its obligatory smoking, but she wouldn't give in.

Having a glass oven door, we could see the puddings cooking, we could see them rising steadily, my smile getting broader, her brows knitting together, and, when the time came to take them out, they stood tall and proud and were as light as a feather! I wish I'd had a camera at that moment as the look on her face was pure gold – in fact,

manufacturers should have paid good money to put her absolutely astounded face on the front of all their packaging – it was the face to launch a million silicone bun sheets!

Out they popped without any sticking to the sides or bottom, served up with lashings of beautiful gravy (as starters in Yorkshire, you don't have them with your actual dinner), and I could see that she was expecting a totally different taste to those done in her old baking tins – but the taste was exactly the same, so it's an old wives' tale that the bakeware gives flavour!

I won the battle on this occasion, but I have to tell you, she still states that you cannot make cakes in silicone! Each to their own – but the 12-hole bun tin still comes out every Sunday regardless of what she says!

What shapes should I buy?

If you're not yet convinced, I would suggest you buy just one piece and give it a 'test drive'. Go for a 12-hole bun mould, as you can use this not only for making buns, to try out your baking results, but also use it for Yorkshire puddings or mini Toads in the Hole.

You can use the same mould to make frozen yogurts or desserts, as, with the mould being so flexible, you just pull the sides away and pop them out.

I use mine for making rice pyramids to go with a curry, as it looks prettier on the plate than a pile of rice, and I also make fridge cakes, such as Rice Krispies buns.

A brilliant idea, if you have small children and are pureeing food (or just want small quantities to use later), pop the food into the 12 holes, pop it

in the freezer and, once frozen, remove them, put them in plastic containers, and you have baby food whenever you need it.

You can even freeze water for ice, as the blocks are small enough to break down for your drinks – just pop one at a time in a plastic bag and bash it with the rolling pin! It's not very scientific but it works! I'm sure you'll discover many other uses for this mould – and that is just one of hundreds of shapes and sizes you can find out there on the High Street.

If you're convinced that silicone is the one for

you, I'd suggest the following pieces would be the most useful for multi-use:

• 2 x round 8 inch cake moulds – you can use these for cakes, but also to roast vegetables, small joints, pies, tarts and quiches. They are also small enough and the right shape to go into the microwave for cooking or re-heating.

• 1 x silicone tray to fit your 12-hole bun mould – handy for placing underneath when transporting liquid for freezing, such as ice cubes, etc. And this can also then be used as a baking tray for your vegetables, chips, cookies, etc.

• 1 x large roasting mould – can be used for general roasting, but also for large, family-sized lasagnes, shepherd's pie, etc. (but remember you cannot put the mould under the grill to brown the topping).

If you stick to these shapes, you'll find many uses for them across all aspects of cooking, from baking to roasting to microwave.

So, will it be goodbye metal, hello silicone? The choice as always is yours, and, as I said before, you may feel happier mixing the two or you may decide silicone isn't for you, but either way, I wish you happy, hassle-free cooking and may your cakes never stick!

Small electricals

There are some electrical items that you should consider, budget allowing, as they not only save energy but are multifunctional and extremely efficient, so those points alone put them high on the list of 'must-haves'. However, don't get carried away at this point into thinking that I am going to let you loose buying all sorts of gadgets – we all know what happened to my so-called 'essential gadget must-haves' – the proof is at the car boot sale and the back of the kitchen cupboards!

THE HALOGEN OVEN
How does it work?
I've been using my halogen oven for several years, and I use it far more than I use the kitchen oven at home. Why? Because it saves energy, it bakes, roasts, steams, grills, and even defrosts in much less time than a conventional oven, and – wait for it – some are even self-clean! How good is that?

When switched on, radiant heat from the

halogen bulb housed under the lid is sent around the circumference of the bowl, at tremendous speed, by a fan also housed on top of the lid.

The temperature control switch lets you control the heat from 20°C right up to 250°C, which is far higher that most conventional ovens. A halogen oven uses up to 60% less energy than a conventional oven, and is up to 35% faster. It's as efficient and cost effective as a microwave, but, unlike a basic microwave, it browns the food like a conventional oven. Halogen heat also renders out the fat during cooking, but at the same time keeps your food moist and succulent.

A good halogen oven has 1300-1400W power, whereas conventional ovens range from 2500-4000W (hence the energy savings).

Benefits of using a halogen oven

You can roast, bake, grill, steam, slow cook, and defrost in a halogen, and, while you're eating your dinner, it also cleans itself! Due to its size, and the fact that all you need to do is plug it in, this portability makes it ideal for the home, caravanning, camping, etc.

The glass bowl never steams up, so you can see your food cooking, and you're always working at counter level – no more bending down to lift things in and out of the oven!

Foods such as meats and fish stay more succulent and juicy than they would in conventional cooking.

The halogen oven is thermostatically controlled, and the light from the halogen bulb will automatically turn off when the required temperature is reached, and turn back on when the temperature drops below the required set temperature.

Most halogen ovens on the market today look identical, and all work in the same way. The halogen oven comprises of a large white plastic base, a borasilica glass bowl (that fits inside the plastic base), a low and high wire cooking rack, a pair of tongs, and a top fitting glass lid which houses the workings of the halogen oven.

The lid fits neatly into the recess of the glass

bowl and houses a handle, a 60-minute timer knob, a temperature control knob, a safety switch that works in conjunction with the handle for switching on and off the power, and a green and red heat and power light.

You can also purchase extra parts for your halogen oven, such as an extender ring for cooking larger foods, a steam tray, and a toast rack, to name but a few.

Tried and tested tips for using the halogen oven
• Ensure there is sufficient space around the halogen oven, as the glass will get hot.

• Never turn the timer knob anti-clockwise as you will damage the oven; just turn off the heat and allow the timer to run its course.

• Whole vegetables will take far longer to cook than meat, such as chops, sausages, etc., so bear this in mind. It's best to part-cook the vegetables first, and then finish them off in the halogen.

• If your food is browning too much, you can either turn the food, cover with a lid, or wrap loosely in foil.

• For healthier eating, cook meats that contain high fat content on the rack supplied, as the excess fats will drip through the bars of the rack and collect at the base of the bowl.

• If using fresh herbs, tuck them under heavier foods or turn the second rack upside down and place on top of the food. This will stop the hot circulating air from blowing the herbs off the surface of the food.

• Rather than using trays, you can use tin foil for wrapping around the cooking racks or for making parcels for steaming fish, meats and vegetables. The steaming process will speed the cooking process of vegetables.

• Purchase a silicon tray (with holes) that fits inside your halogen oven on the top cooking rack. This is ideal for cooking chips and smaller foods, and also allows the hot circulating air to penetrate through to the underside of chips making them crispy all round.

• For searing and grilling food, use the high cooking rack, at temperatures between 220-250° – fantastic for steaks, chicken wings, sausages, bacon, pizzas and garlic bread.

• The low cooking rack is best used for all roasts, casseroles, baking, steaming, and defrosting.

• Finally, don't be afraid to experiment when you're cooking, and when you've mastered the halogen oven I'm sure that you'll agree that it's the best piece of equipment you ever bought!

INDUCTION HOBS
This is another fantastic invention on my list of 'must-haves'. You can use it in your kitchen at home, instead of or as well as your current hob (a real boon when cooking for larger numbers), but can take it away with you to your caravan, as long as you have an electric hook up, or your holiday home.

Induction hobs are great if you like to cook speedily, and are easy to clean as it's the pan that heats up, not the hob itself, so spills don't burn onto the surface.

atmosphere, and, if you use ceramic, you lose more than that, which means that you're heating the pan and the kitchen, too! The savings on your energy bill is enormous, so an induction hob is certainly worth considering.

However, before we go any further, let's talk about how an induction hob works, as, once you understand this, you'll see why having one would be such an advantage.

How does induction work?

Within the main body of the hob is an element which, when the hob is plugged in, produces a high frequency electromagnetic field. Covering this element is a cooking surface made from glass ceramic, so there's no 'open flame' to worry about.

In order for the element to work when you place a pan onto the hob, you need cookware with

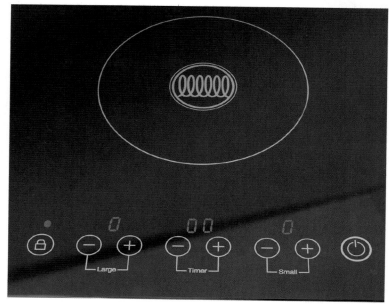

The great thing about induction cooking is that it is super-efficient, from an energy using point of view. The heat is transferred directly to the pan itself, so little energy is lost. Over 95% of the heat is taken in by the pan. On other heat sources, such as gas, you lose around 50% of the heat into the

strength of this electromagnetic field instantly, so there's no waiting for it to change temperature as there is with an ceramic hob, for example. You can lower the heat to 40°C, turning it into a slow cooker, or raise it to a maximum of 220°C, which is just what you need when wok cooking or searing meat.

Anything outside of the pan itself is not affected by the magnetic field, and, as soon as the pan is lifted off the hob, the heat element stops completely after one minute. There is some residual heat from the area where the pan has been, but it's not particularly hot as it's the pan that holds the heat – indeed, the area around the hob will be cool to the touch.

When I'm demonstrating, people are absolutely amazed when they see me cooking a pan full of bubbling hot food whilst a piece of chocolate sits on the hob, keeping perfect shape and not melting at all! It takes some believing I know, but again, I must emphasise that it is the *pan* that gets hot, *not* the hob. This feature makes it a very safe way to cook, and is why I always use an induction hob whilst I am demonstrating, particularly when there are children involved, as the possibility of burn injuries is significantly less than with other heat sources. When you're finished cooking, a damp cloth over the surface will clean up any spills so your hob will stay looking good.

Overall, an induction hob is a good buy – clean, efficient, energy-saving, safe, and as an added bonus, portable, so it's perfect if you're off to camping or caravan sites, or if you're sending your teenager to university where the cooking facilities can be somewhat lacking. You just need a 13 amp electric socket and away you go!

As an aside, I was in a store in Scotland once, and

a magnetic base (see the chapter on cookware for more details). If the cookware is compatible (and many are these days), the electromagnetism penetrates the base, setting up a circulating electrical current, which in turn generates heat. The heat generated in the pan is transferred to the food inside the pan but not to any other area outside of the base of the pan.

With just a push of a button you can control the

a chap who was listening to my presentation of the induction hob piped up, "Enough laddie, I'll take four! I am a carpenter so I can build them into my kitchen work top and, when we go away in our camper van every weekend with the wife, I can take two out and take them with us." What a great idea, I thought, and the remaining customers all thought so too – I sold another four on the strength of this man and his camper van.

When I returned to the same store some six months later, the chap was again there and asked to buy another two hobs. "Two more?" I asked, "... did you have a problem with the ones I sold you last time?" "No laddie," he replied, "... they are working well – it's the missus that's the problem – she cannot bear the thought of having two gaping holes in her worktop every time we take them out to go in the campervan, so I am having to buy two more," and he turned on his heel, a hob under each arm and went on his way. I have been back to that store many times but I haven't seen him since!

To see a video of how an induction hob works and all its benefits, visit www.melandmal.com and go to Videos.

WHAT ELSE SHOULD I CONSIDER?
This is where you have to blindfold yourself when you go into a kitchen department, as what looks like a great idea at the time, can often turn out not to be when it finds itself at the back of the cupboard through lack of use!

So, here are my top four gadgets that you will use time and time again, and really get your money's worth:

- Mini chopper: Small, compact, and very easy to

use for all sorts of jobs, including mincing small foodstuffs such as onions and garlic, grinding coffee beans, and zapping up breadcrumbs.

Being small, you can pop this in a cupboard as it takes up hardly any space at all – a real bonus if you are limited to where you can store things. Cleaning by hand is simple and quick as it has so few parts, unlike the larger food processors.

Our mini chopper is in use several times a week, and you will find it a great little helper when you are cooking and need a job done quickly and efficiently with little mess.

Look for one around the £50 mark, as these have a more powerful motor and are better quality than the less expensive versions.

• Handheld mixer: Whisking egg whites for meringues or beating the butter and sugar together

when making a cake is very hard work by hand, and also time consuming, as you have to keep stopping to give your arm a break! So, this item makes these tedious jobs so much less hassle.

A mixer will whisk, mix, whip, beat and combine foods very quickly, with the added bonus that it is that is light, portable and small, so very easy to house in a cupboard when not in use.

have had one for over 20 years, used several times a week, and it is still going strong, so buy the best you can afford.

When you have finished the job, simply press a button to eject the beaters, wash them by hand or in the dishwasher, and wipe over the mixer section with a damp cloth.

Handhelds are brilliant if you are doing small quantities, but if you are a regular baker and make larger amounts of cake mix, or you make your own bread which takes a longer kneading time, then I would highly recommend that you invest in a good stand-alone mixer. However, for day-to-day food preparation, a handheld version should be sufficient.

- Stick blender: A quick and easy way to puree food, make wonderful smoothies, and blend soups and sauces, even when they are still in the pan. Unless you have a liquidizer or a stand-alone mixer, which can be very costly if you buy good ones, plus they take up valuable space in either your cupboards or on the counter top, a stick blender item is a must in the kitchen. The blending part is housed in the end of the unit and you simply put this into the food and press a button. It is easy to use, easy to clean and very inexpensive, and, being slim, you can put this in a drawer as easily as putting away a pair of tongs or a spatula. Once you have one, you'll find many uses for it, so keep it to hand!

- Slow cooker: If you work during the day, or just want a day out without slaving away over your hob, but want something delicious to come home to, then a slow cooker is one of the best things you will buy. Simply put all your ingredients – meat ,vegetables and liquid – into the ceramic dish, pop on the lid,

They are generally sold with at least two sets of stainless steel whisks, and have various speed settings from slow to very fast. As it's handheld, you're able to control the speed with a simple press of a button, and move the beaters round the bowl to ensure that all the ingredients are mixed properly. Try to get one with a motor around 250 watts, as this will give you better results and will last longer. I

plug it in and turn the control knob to cook, and it will bubble away all day completely unattended. Some have thermostats to bring the food to a specific temperature, then lower it again, but one with a simple low/high heat is sufficient to do a good job. Timers are useful if you intend being out longer than eight hours, which is the average time to cook a good pot full of food, but even without a timer, your food will be perfectly fine if there's enough liquid in it from the start of the cooking time – the liquid evaporates in the process so more liquid is better, and you can always thicken it at the end of the cooking time with a teaspoon of cornflour.

Slow cookers are perfect if you want to use cheaper cuts of meat, such as stewing meat or mutton, as the long cooking times soften the often chewy sinews, making the meat extremely tender, and gives a delicious flavour to your food. Most good units come with a small recipe book to give you an idea of cooking times for different foods, along with an instruction manual.

There are various capacities available, so ensure that you buy one to suit your everyday needs according to how many you're cooking for. For example, if you're mostly cooking for a family of four, then a 3.5L is a good size. To save time and energy, why not make double quantity, utilize the cooker's maximum capacity, and freeze what you don't eat for another day. If you have limited strength in your arms or wrists, you might find a smaller version better for you.

Best of all, by cooking in just one pot, you have less washing up to do!

THE MICROWAVE

In the next chapter I talk about microwave cookware but you need a microwave first!

You may be asking why on earth do I need one? Many people believe that it is nothing more than a glorified food warmer or defroster, but this couldn't be further from the truth. In fact, many recipe books give timings for using a microwave as well as the conventional methods of cooking, as the same results can be reached more quickly.

There is just so much that you can do quickly in a microwave that would take an age in an oven or on the hob, such as cooking fish, steaming vegetables, making light and fluffy omelettes, cooking delicate meats such as chicken or duck, or simply preparing the fruit for a crumble dessert. They retain nutrients, flavour and the colour of your food, and best of all, save money on energy bills!

Before you rush out and buy one, consider the size of your kitchen and where you are going to put it, as this will dictate the physical size to look for. This is one of those appliances, a bit like your kettle, that you will always have out on your countertop, so it needs to fit in neatly.

What are you going to use it for? If you're going to cook in it rather than just reheat or defrost foods, then you will need a medium to high wattage, around 700-850W, with a rotating turntable, as this ensures that your food will cook evenly.

Think about the size of the inside of the microwave as well as the outside, as it has to be large enough to take larger dishes as well as small. Whether there is one of you or a family, I would always advocate opting for a medium to large size, as there's more scope for cooking larger quantities if you should need to.

Personally, I prefer microwaves with an LED touch panel rather than a dial as it gives you a precise timing rather than just approximate. This is very important if you're following a recipe when just a few seconds either way can result in undercooked or overcooked food.

All microwaves have the facility to cook on full power or lesser powers for simmering or defrosting.

To use the microwave to its full potential, it is important that the one you choose does have these options as standard.

Of course, you can buy microwaves on the internet, but I would always suggest that you go to a store to look at a selection first. Check that it is the right size and wattage, that the inside is large enough for cooking for a family, and the controls are easy to use and easy to read. When you've done your homework and you know what is right for you, surf the internet to your heart's content knowing that what you buy is exactly what you need. It may seem time consuming but when you are parting with your cash, of course, it's worth the extra effort.

Microwave cookware

Many homes have a microwave in the kitchen; they're as common as an oven or a hob top, such is their popularity in recent years. With our fast-paced lives, we enjoy the speed and convenience that microwave cooking can give us.

As I said in the last chapter, microwaves are fantastic if you're looking for fast cooking, reheating or defrosting. However, unlike conventional ovens, they do not naturally brown and crisp foods, unless you use specific pieces of equipment to give you that oven-cooked finish. Vegetables steamed in the microwave retain many of the vitamins that otherwise can be lost if cooked in water on the hob.

Whether you are cooking for one or more, there is no doubt that a microwave is a valuable asset to any kitchen, if only for doing the basics, such as cooking baked potatoes, to heat ready meals, or reheat or defrost food.

That's not to say that you cannot make a whole meal in a microwave, but most people these days use a microwave in conjunction with an oven or hob top and get the best of both worlds.

WHAT EQUIPMENT DO I NEED?
In reality, probably much of what you could use in a microwave is already sat in your cupboards, but there are rules that you must follow to prevent problems.

Silicone, plastic, heat resistant glass, pottery or ceramic dishes or containers are all good materials to use in a microwave.

Metal items cannot be put into a basic microwave as this causes the microwaves to 'arc'. This will appear as flashes of light on the metal item, be it a baking tray, or tin foil, or even crockery with a silver or gold edging around it.

If you're using ceramic or glass bowls and dishes, try to use round items as opposed oval or square, so that it's the same shape as the turntable, as this makes for more even cooking. You can cover the dish with cling-film when cooking, or use a plate cover to stop spattering during cooking. If you opt for silicone, you will find that any shape which fits the turntable inside the microwave will be perfect.

If you're using a storage container that comes with a lid, take care not to fasten the lid down, but only place it gently on top. The steam from cooking the food needs to escape, otherwise a vacuum will build up and you won't be able to get the lid off without piercing it to release the steam, which can be dangerous.

Silicone items may come with lids which are perforated so that vacuums are not a problem.

Whilst using a dish or a bowl is common practice, there are ranges of microwave cookware that are made specifically for the job, and are very useful. I would recommend that you invest in a few pieces, as they are relatively inexpensive.

Try to buy decent quality microwave-ware as this will last far longer than some of the less expensive items you can find in most stores these days. The best ones are those made from clear polycarbonate. This is very tough, stain-proof, non-stick, freezer-proof, and dishwasher-safe, although my favourite is silicone but you know that already!

Such is the variety of microwave cookware available in stores, you may be tempted to buy far more than you need. Don't get carried away, as you still have to store them somewhere! From experience, I'd recommend only a few pieces, of sizes that suit your needs, and that you will use day in, day out.

POLYCARBONATE MICROWAVE-WARE
- A small saucepan with lid – you can use this for cooking baked beans, peas, carrots, soup – just

about anything in small quantities, and the lid will stop any spattering during cooking and keep your microwave pristine.

- An omelette maker – just whisk the egg mixture and pour into the mould, pop the lid down and let the microwave do its job. You get a perfectly fluffy omelette in just a few minutes, and it comes out in a folded omelette shape, too!

• Jacket potato tray/bacon crisper – this is in constant use in our kitchen, as potatoes take only a third of the time they would in the oven. The potato just sits on the raised nodules, allowing the microwaves to cook and crisp all the way round. You can also use it as a bacon crisper, so if you're watching your weight, or just don't want the hassle of using the grill or a frying pan (and having to wash it afterwards), this ribbed tray cooks and crisps bacon beautifully, and all the fats drain away.

• Multi-steamer – this makes perfectly fluffy rice and steamed vegetables, whilst retaining all the colour and vitamins during the cooking process.

• And finally, a plate cover – you can use your silicone splatter guard, as I mentioned in the silicone chapter, but check that it's microwave-proof first. This is a cover with sides on, so that you can pop it on top of your plate or bowl – saving all the hassle of covering it with clingfilm – and eliminating the mess of splattered food in your microwave. Easy to clean and can be stored inside the microwave when not in use.

SILICONE

• An oval silicone steamer is really worth having as you can cook not only delicate foods, such as salmon, in it, but also long vegetables, such as sliced runner beans, courgettes and asparagus. I also use mine for cooking omelettes – just pour in the mix, pop on the lid, microwave for a couple of minutes, and I have a wonderfully tasty and fluffy supper dish.

• A silicone steamer, square or round, with lid. You can cook just about anything you want in these, from a selection of vegetables to a full Thai curry, they are so versatile. Having rigid handles they are easy to move about safely, even when full, and, as mentioned earlier, the lids are slightly perforated to ensure that there's not a strong vacuum formed. Don't forget that steaming is a very healthy way of cooking, so these are an excellent idea if you are watching your weight!

Microwaves are not everyone's choice, but they are quick and convenient. However, you do not have to sacrifice quality for speed – just buy the right equipment and you will get excellent results and reap the benefits of this type of cooking.

Food storage

I'm not a betting man but I wouldn't mind guessing that if you went into your kitchen right now, and opened the door on your so-called storage container cupboard, either everything would fall out, or it's full of plastic take-way containers! And the reason I know that I would win my bet is that our kitchen cupboard was exactly the same, and there are millions of others like it across the length and breadth of the country!

I don't know why, but we seem to have this obsession with saving butter, ice-cream and takeaway containers, in the belief that they're going to keep our food fresher for longer. Of course, you can keep food covered inside them, but they're not airtight, watertight, microwaveable, freezer-proof, or dishwasher-proof, and, therefore, not really doing the job of food storage in the true sense of the word.

All we really need is some good quality, food grade, re-useable plastic containers that we can use in the larder, fridge, freezer and the microwave, that really do keep fresh food fresher for longer, can be used for left-overs, and will eliminate food wastage. Food is a very expensive commodity, so you need to use every last bit of it. Ask yourself how often how you take a piece of cheese out of its wrapper and then cover it loosely in foil or cling film, only to find that it has gone dry or is starting to go mouldy within only a few days, or that lettuce you put in the fridge yesterday is already looking rather limp today – and then you end up throwing it away.

The trouble is that without a little guidance, you could soon end up with a cupboard full of wonderful storage containers with nothing in them, and wondering what to do with them all! So, it's worth thinking about how you would use them – it's all back to doing your homework again before you step out of the front door!

It's all very well me talking to you about storing things in plastic containers, and extolling their virtues, but you have to know that until I started presenting them on shopping channels, I was the world's worst for unwrapping a hunk of cheese and then leaving it open in the fridge (then complaining when I went back for more and it had dried out, like it wasn't my fault!). I also used to open a can, eat half the contents, and then put the can into the fridge so it could oxidize nicely and the food go off; yikes! The health and hygiene inspector would have had me locked up!

However, I'm pleased to report that I am now a reformed character, firstly from constantly using and being totally reliant on these little plastic boxes to do my job as a demonstrator and presenter, but most of all from the strict training regime that my wife Mel put me into several years ago, and is currently running with our teenage son who seems to have a mental block where 'putting things away safely' is concerned. He takes milk out of the fridge, but doesn't put it back, puts cheese containers back in the fridge, but without their lids ... get the picture?

He'll get it eventually, probably when he is about to leave home ... at 30.

So, the message is, start training them as soon as they can open the fridge or cupboard door!

WHAT SHOULD I BE LOOKING FOR WHEN BUYING FOOD STORAGE CONTAINERS?

If you go into any cookshop or look on the internet, you'll be met with a huge array of storage containers, of various shapes and sizes, and made from glass or plastic (or both), with or without locking devices, with vacuum pumps, or just plain push-on lids.

The main thing to look for is that the container clearly states that it can be safely used in fridge,

100% STACKABLE AIRTIGHT CONTAINER

...ABSOLUTELY AIR TIGHT
...LIQUID TIGHT
...DISHWASHER &
MICROWAVE SAFE

Open the lid in microwave oven.
Only re-heatable, not for cooking.

freezer or cupboard, is airtight, watertight, microwaveable and dishwashersafe. If it says this, then you'll be able to put foods that are dry, wet, raw, cooked or liquids into these containers without any fear of leakage or spoilage.

The best containers by far, in my opinion, are those which incorporate a silicone seal into the lid, so when the locks are pushed down, the silicone expands, ensuring that the box is indeed all the things it says it is on the packaging.

Lids with locking devices do tend to give a better seal, and this is very important if you're transporting foods.

HOW CAN I USE THESE CONTAINERS?
There are so many uses, I could go on forever but the main uses are:

- Storing raw foods and fresh foods in the same fridge, eliminating cross-contamination of foods and odours.

- For left-overs.

- Freezing foods, either pre-cooked or raw.

- Bulk cooking so that you can make more than you need and save some for another day and another meal.

- Reheating foods.

- Making portions of baby food.

- As lunch boxes for school and work.

- For transporting food to the elderly or someone in hospital.

- For cat and dog food (mark the box so that you know it is for pets only!).

Once you have decided what you might use them for, my first tip is to buy only a few at a time – avoid large sets of containers as there are always sizes within the pack that you just will not use. It may look cheaper to buy in sets but it's false economy. Far better to buy single items that you know you will use, and that will not clutter up your cupboards.

In the fridge
Food safety is very important. We all store dairy, raw and cooked foods in this one place, even if they are on different shelves. I cannot emphasise enough

how important it is that foods are stored separately to avoid cross contamination, so putting them into airtight and watertight containers is the best way to avoid this.

For example, how often have you opened the fridge door and your eyes have watered as the odour from particularly smelly cheeses hits you? These smells do permeate other foods, particularly eggs which are very porous, so putting these foods into airtight containers will eliminate this and keep your fridge smelling fresh.

Your fridge will also stay cleaner for longer if everything is housed in a container – no leakages, spills or juices dripping from one shelf to another. Everything safe, neat and well organised.

In the larder

Flour, pasta, sugar, coffee, tea, rice, biscuits and other dry foods all need to be stored in the correct containers once the packets have been opened. If they aren't, not only will the foodstuff deteriorate very quickly, but ants, weevils and other nasties can get into the food – not a pleasant experience to any one who has ever experienced that!

There are always sell by dates on dry foods, and what I find useful is cutting the sell by information off the packet and popping it into the container itself as a point of reference. You could also label the container with the sell by date on it. This will give you an indication of what needs using first, helping you organize your food rotation. The kitchen is one of the most common places for encountering food poisoning, which is why you'll always find very high standards of food storage in a professional kitchen, and you should do the same at home. That's food for thought!

As there are different types of flour and they all look the same once out of their packaging, you might want to labels your containers, to highlight exactly what sort of flour each contains.

Food storage in the freezer

I would always suggest that you use containers that specifically say they are for use in the freezer, as these won't split or crack under the extremely low temperatures. Not only will your food be contained safely, it will avoid any 'freezer burn', which is common if you just use any old plastic container, foil or clingfilm.

Being watertight is also very important if you need to store liquids; soups and sauces, for example. It can get a bit messy otherwise!

Having a freezer allows you to buy foodstuffs in bulk, thus saving money. Eat what you need, then freeze the rest for another day. Alternatively, if you like to cook in bulk, just put portions into one or more containers and get them out when you're ready to cook.

When it comes to thawing out food in the microwave, you can do so in the container itself if it's microwaveable. The lids on good quality containers can be taken off easily, even when frozen, so that you can see what's in the container without having to thaw the food first. It's a good idea to label the box before you put it in the freezer – I have often taken out what I thought was a lasagne and then, once it had thawed, found it to be just raw mince; very annoying!

If you have babies and puree food for them, buying the mini containers which are large enough for one portion, means you can puree to your heart's content! Just store those for quick use in the fridge

and put the rest in the freezer. My wife used to do this when our son was small, and it meant that all she had to do was thaw and reheat – one happy baby!

In the microwave
Check the packaging to make sure that the containers are microwaveable. If not, they could melt, and the plastic will warp, particularly the lids which then will no longer fit the box. If you're certain they're suitable for microwave use, you can even take them straight from the freezer to thaw the contents in the microwave, or, if you just want to warm something up, you don't have to take it out of the container first.

It is important to unlock the lid first, when re-heating or thawing in the microwave, as otherwise a vacuum will form and it will be impossible to get the lid off without damaging it. Once you've unlocked it, place it lightly back on top so it acts as a splatter shield.

In the dishwasher
If this is a consideration for you, make sure that you check out the packaging before you buy. Most good quality plastic containers are suitable for dishwashers, usually on the top shelf. If not, just wash in warm soapy water and either allow to air dry, or dry them thoroughly before you put on the

lid ready for the next batch of food, particularly if storing dry foods.

What shapes and sizes should I buy?
This all depends on what conclusion you came to when you were considering how you would use them, but these are the ones that we use constantly:

• At least two rectangular-shaped containers, large enough to hold a pack of butter or a wedge of cheese. These can then be used for storing just about anything, from raw chicken breasts to salads.

• A long rectangular bacon box, as this can be used for other foods, such as spring onions, celery, etc.

• A set of round bowls, for storing or mixing ingredients in, then cooking in the microwave; useful for when making an omelette or scrambled egg.

• Three taller containers to hold flour, sugar, rice, or tea and coffee.
• Two very tall containers to hold dried pasta, including spaghetti.

• A cereal box with a flip top lid. This can also be used for flour, small pasta, etc.

• Three or four mini boxes; great for storing dried herbs or for the baby food I mentioned earlier.

If you're a baker and need storage for flour, sugar, dried fruit, etc., the tall containers would be perfect, so you might want to invest in more of these. Alternatively, if you have a family who like a choice of cereal for breakfast, you might want more than one cereal container. It really is up to you, of course, but if you think about what you really need before you surf the internet or visit the shops, you'll buy wisely and know that you're going to use what you purchase day after day, and won't just clutter up your precious cupboard space. If your storage containers take up more than one shelf in your kitchen, you have too many!

As an aside, watch out for the men in your house, as they have a tendency to pinch these little storage boxes for their sheds and garages. Many a plastic container has ended up being used to house nuts and bolts, screws or golf tees! So, ladies, you might want to consider buying a set for the man in your life, too!

Adding to your collection

Having followed the advice in the foregoing chapters, you should be forming a picture in your mind of kitchen cupboards full of equipment that you are actually going to use on a day-to-day basis, with everything seeing the light of day at least once a week! There should be nothing gathering dust at the back of a drawer – if there is, you've strayed off the 'Kitchenware Path'!

At some point, after you have kept to buying only the basics, you'll be bitten by the 'kitchen gadget bug' and will start asking yourself 'what else can I add to my collection'? This is where you have to stop and take exactly the line of action we've taken all through this book – are you really going to use it if you do buy it?

Let's look at each of the categories ... here are some things that you may want to consider ...

COOKWARE
* A maslin pan – if you are into preserving jams or

chutneys, then you'll need one of these. Maslin pans are open-topped pans with a handle (a bit like a half-sized bucket, and around 18 inches in diameter), and are available in either aluminium or stainless steel. They can be used on most heat sources.

Personally, I prefer the stainless steel version as it's more robust, although there's no difference in the performance whichever you choose.

Look for a maslin pan with a capacity of 9 litres (any larger and you wont be able to lift it when it's full).

Maslin pans can also be used for making large quantities of soup, stews or curries on the hob top, but use a lid or splatter guard over the top in the cooking process or you'll end up with a messy cooker!

• Cast iron ribbed skillet – a really useful addition to your current selection of pots and pans as this can be used instead of a frying pan. Use it on the hob top or barbeque for steaks, burgers, sausages, etc. I find this a great pan for cooking and searing meat or vegetables. The ribbed surface leaves a

pattern on the meat, and catches all the fat so that it can be drained away; so much better for your waistline!

KNIVES
The following knives can be add to your basic collection; all are useful in their own way:

• Bread knife: the serrated edge helps to cut

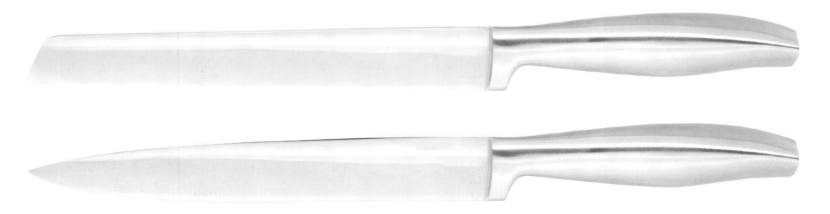

garlic and ginger. This is a very much preferred piece of equipment for chefs involved in Sushi and Chinese cooking – in fact, a very famous Chinese chef very kindly gave me a cleaver when I was working with him at a trade show. Lovely man, I think he even made us a cup of tea!

KITCHEN UTENSILS

When you are looking around a cookshop, there's bound to be something that you think is a really good idea, and you will be tempted – believe me, I've been there … many times! Think before you buy, though, even if the item costs only a few pounds. Avoid it if you're going to take it out of the drawer only on the odd occasion – this will stop you buying items such as a butter curler!

However, there are some items that we use in our house on a pretty regular basis, so you might want to consider these:

• Pastry cutters – usually in mixed sets, some with a fluted edge, some with plain. We use the plain ones when baking scones, but also for keeping fried eggs

through crusty loaves without tearing the soft inside.

• Carving knife – a long slender knife with a slight curve on the blade, used to carve meat.

• Boning knife – a slender blade about a quarter of an inch in depth, solely designed for boning meat and poultry.

• Filleting knife – great for skinning fish.

• Meat cleaver – a large heavy knife, very deep sides, rectangular in shape, and a thick spine. Suitable for chopping through bones and tendons. The sides of the cleaver can be used for squashing

into the juices, release the bulb and the juices will be sucked into the tube – then just squeeze the bulb again to release the liquid and baste away! Simple but ingenious!

• Piping bags and nozzles – essential if you enjoy decorating cakes, etc., but also very useful when piping mashed potatoes on the top of a shepherd's pie!

• Jar opener – if you struggle to open jars, this gadget is worth having in your drawer. Just place the circular holder around the top of the lid, turn the jar and the lid will release easily. More efficient that tapping the side of the lid with a knife, running it under the hot tap, or swearing at it!

BAKEWARE
A few little extras but not imperatives:

• 14 inch round pizza tray – this gets a lot of use in our house, as it can be used for pizza, garlic bread, or chips, and, having holes in its base, the heat gets right underneath the food, ensuring your pizza base is crispy and your chips are golden all the way round; no more soggy bottoms!

• An eight inch loose-bottomed flan dish – for flans, quiches, cheesecakes, etc. I'm not saying that you will have this out every day, but the moment you want to make a flan, you will regret not having one, as you just push the flan out from the bottom, giving a perfectly formed pastry case and filling.

SMALL ELECTRICALS
Unless you are into cooking or baking in a big way,

round when cooking (only when we have guests for breakfast, first impressions are everything!).

• Baster – or as we call it in our house, a 'gravy sucker', thus named by our then three year old and it has stuck ever since. This little gadget is perfect for basting chickens, turkeys, or joints in the oven, without having to take them out. Essentially a large syringe, with a plastic open tube with a silicone bulb on one end – squeeze the bulb, put the other end

the list of products suggested in Chapter 7 should cover all the bases, and perhaps it would be best if you work with what you have for a few weeks or months before buying anything else. Remember, even the smallest piece of electrical equipment can be expensive, so only buy what you know you're missing.

MICROWAVE COOKWARE

If you browse the internet or step into a cookshop, I'm sure there will be products that will tempt you, but I think there's only so much microwave equipment you will really use on a daily basis. It might not be expensive but it can take up a lot of space in your cupboards!

FOOD STORAGE

The basic shapes we discussed should be sufficient, but you may find that you have specific needs so buy accordingly. For example, if you do a lot of baking, you might prefer flip-top caddies so that you can scoop out ingredients rather than having to undo the locking hinges. You will need to tailor your purchases to your own needs, and you do need to take this into consideration when buying your 'basics' in the first place.

And that's it ... I hope you've enjoyed your journey with me, and that you've picked up some useful information along the way. As I have reiterated constantly, whatever you decide to add to your collection, ensure that you're going to use it! Otherwise, you'll end up in the same situation as you were in before you read this book! Full cupboards, overflowing with stuff that hasn't seen the light of day in years, with a lot wasted space and, more importantly, wasted money.

Take a good look through whatever you have already got and decide whether it will do the job. If so, that's great news, as it means you can save your money for something else. However, if you've not used an item for several months (years even?), get rid of it – do a car boot sale and raise money for your brand spanking new kitchen equipment. Alternatively, flog it to your unsuspecting friends who haven't yet read this book (but suggest they buy a copy when their cupboards are full of unused stuff!), or simply donate to your local charity shop. Whatever you do, do it NOW!

Once you have the right equipment, it's time to put it into action!

Coming soon, a series of colour recipe books covering a variety of foods and equipment as discussed here.

For more information, please visit us on our website melandmal.com

Cook Equipped Part 1

Malcolm Harradine

My second book, Cook Equipped Part 1 follows on from this one, and shows you wonderful recipes can produce using all those pieces of cookware, bakeware, and utensils that fill your kitchen cupboards.

Packed with 'Technique Teach-in' reference pages, together with full colour recipes, many my very own creations, I will guide you through using your equipment to its full potential, preparing food for family and friends, with hints and tips plus an added section dedicated to kids cooking.

Cook Equipped Part 2

Malcolm Harradine

More from Malcolm Harradine's collection, helping you to improve your preparation and cooking skills with his new book Cook Equipped Part 2. Introducing more 'Technique Teach-ins', with instructions and photographs to help you master more varied tasks, and suggestions to increase your kitchen collection, plus a brand new collection of recipes and hints and tips to take you to the next level.

Index

A Kitchen Equipped